YOU'RE TELLING MY KIDS THEY CAN'T READ THIS BOOK?

Our Hundred-Year
Children's-Literature Revolution
and How We'll Keep Fighting to
Support Our Families' Right to Read

ANDREW LATIES

Cataloging in Publication Data
Library of Congress Control Number: 2025910198

Laties, Andrew
 You're telling my kids they can't read this book? our hundred-year children's-literature revolution and how we'll keep fighting to support our families' right to read / Andrew Laties

ISBN 979-8-9908448-5-8 (pbk)
ISBN 979-8-9908448-6-5 (ebook)

1. Literary Criticism—Children's & Young Adult Literature
2. Political Science—Censorship
3. Booksellers—United States
4. Biography & Autobiography—Memoirs
5. Laties, Andrew

The events and conversations in this book have been set down to the best of the author's ability.

Cover design: Gaia Abraxas
Back jacket photo: Joan Zachary
Printed and bound in the United States of America

First printing July 1, 2025
Published by Rebel Bookseller, an imprint of Book and Puppet Company, Easton, PA, USA, 18042

PASSIONATELY FIGHTING BOOK-BANNING AND CENSORSHIP: HOW & WHY

In this timely broadside against censorship, Laties weaves together stories from his fifty years as a bookseller, activist, and parent, while sharing tales from authors, librarians, publishers, journalists, and customers. Discussing events as recent as the May 2025 firing of the Librarian of Congress and the June 2025 Supreme Court LGBTQ+ storybook decision, this conversational book reveals patterns in the history of book challenges, while teaching resistance tactics. An essential read for parents, librarians, educators, and everyone committed to intellectual freedom.

"At a time when the American government and right-wing organizations claim to set moral standards for children by banning numerous books and destroying libraries and bookstores, Andrew Laties exposes their hypocrisy. A must read for anyone troubled by the plight in America when groups of adults want to dumb down children. Laties has fought and continues to fight oppressive guardians of ignorance, and his book reveals that his fight is our fight."—Jack Zipes, author, *Buried Treasures: The Power of Political Fairy Tales;* Professor Emeritus, University of Minnesota

"A rapid-fire history of the politics of book-banning, the complicated issues surrounding censorship, and a how-to guide on launching a book fair, laced throughout with an emphatic call to action to preserve our freedom of expression at a time of unprecedented governmental attacks on it."
—Paul Gulino, author, *Screenwriting: The Sequence Approach;* Professor, Chapman University

"Really wonderful! Powerful, poignant with dashes of humor. Well written—the narrative barrels along—lucid yet profound. An important read in these treacherous times."—H. Nichols B. Clark, co-author, *Myth, Magic, and Mystery: One Hundred Years of American Children's Book Illustration;* Founding Director & Chief Curator Emeritus, The Eric Carle Museum of Picture Book Art

For Gaia Abraxas

Contents

PRELUDE—ASSIGNMENT FROM MELBA

"You're all correspondents, and this is your assignment," announces Melba Tolliver, the legendary New York City journalist who in 1967 was the first Black person to anchor a national newscast: "Report on something that happened this week in your everyday life, which no-one else knows about."

It's 5:30pm on Sunday, January 26th, 2025. Just last Monday, on Donald Trump's Inauguration Day, Melba hosted a four-hour community read-aloud of Special Counsel Jack Smith's report about Trump's actions during the January 6th, 2021 assault on the Capitol; dozens of neighbors took turns presenting. Our program got a full write-up from a *Morning Call* newspaper journalist. At today's follow-up program, Melba Tolliver has been teaching principles from George Lakoff's manual for resistance, *Don't Think of an Elephant! Know Your Values and Frame the Debate*. Twenty-five customers have again turned out. But now, halfway through the hour, Melba has turned the tables by challenging us to become journalists ourselves.

This assignment should be pretty easy, but from my spot at the back of the bookstore, I can see none of our attendees are raising their hands with a report.

"Come on!" challenges Melba. "Everyone has something to say about the past week!"

Impulsively, I come to the rescue of my shy clientele; I speak up. "I have something."

The two-dozen heads swivel one-eighty degrees, and I launch into the story I just remembered. "I signed up for a book industry workshop two weeks ago: a bunch of booksellers were on a Zoom call. Our association was helping us plan our marketing schedules for the year. I saw on the Zoom screen the face of a fellow bookseller who I knew from social media had closed a location. During a moment when we were allowed to chat, I expressed condolence. But my colleague looked more angry than sad and said, 'Didn't you hear? That store depends on bookfairs and orders from schools for about half its income. Some people demanded the district shouldn't work with us because of books we carry and what we stand for. They put enough pressure through social media and parents' groups, so the educators felt the situation was 'too volatile' to keep hosting bookfairs. That was the final straw.'"

As I recounted this conversation, I could see that the customers in my store were shocked. Several cried out in anger. I continued, "Wait, there's more. The next day, I returned to the weeklong workshop, and that bookseller wasn't on the Zoom. When I mentioned to the others who had returned how I hadn't known the true tale of the bookstore's closing, a different bookseller had said, 'Yesterday, you didn't hear the whole story. Guys were in front of the store with AR-15 rifles.'"

Melba Tolliver now took over. "Andy! Has this been reported anywhere?"

"No," I said, "And I doubt my colleague would want it covered. We're running bookstores and we want people to associate us with positive stuff—we don't want bad publicity. It's just an accident that I learned the truth."

Melba—who at eighty-six years old is suffering from various ailments, but still insists that she is not retired, but rather "rewired"—responded, "This is exactly the journalist's job. Some stories would never become known because their subjects would rather keep quiet. Your assignment is to research this story some more and report to us with background in two weeks."

Several of my customers began to speak up, suggesting tasks for me. "Give a phone call and get more facts!" "Talk with the school district!" "Tell the media!"

But I knew I wouldn't do any of those things, because I had learned the story in a confidential way—a professional context. In this colleague's divided community I could damage the remaining bookselling operation if I forced this ugly story into public view.

A few weeks later, a young couple who spoke to each other in German were browsing in the bookstore. The woman asked me a question: "We have heard of book-banning in America. Is this something you know about?"

"Oh, sure," I answered. "It's a big problem."

"And, what books are they banning?"

"Well, lots. There are some national groups that circulate lists to local groups. People take the lists to schools and demand those books be removed."

She repeated her question, "But what are the books?"

"Well, just look around. My bookstore has banned books." I gestured at a children's Black-Interest section right behind her. "Lots of the books in this case are banned, for instance. Or—" I stepped over to another case and plucked a hardback copy of *And Tango Makes Three*. "Here," I said, handing her the book. "This is one of the most banned books in America."

The two of them examined the charming image of three penguins on the cover, and the man asked, "Why is this banned?"

"Well, it's a true story about two penguins at the zoo—two male penguins—who raise a baby penguin. A true story. About animals. But it's banned because the book-banners object to same-sex people raising children. I mean, it's not even a metaphorical fairy tale—this is a true story about penguins, animal behavior."

"Okay, I'll buy it," the man announced.

Book-banning goes back thousands of years and includes what can only be called crimes against humanity, like the Spanish Inquisition's systematic destruction of the massive Aztec, Maya, and Inca literatures. In the modern era, the Nazi book-burnings of the 1930's are front-of-mind. Such wholesale book-destruction is not what the United States is experiencing now. Today's performative book-banning, from school board to courtroom, is a battle tactic in our culture war.

We've been fighting censorship in the United States for years, and we have always beaten it back. Hearing stories of past success can encourage our efforts and offer lessons.

I'm doing my assignment, Melba.

1-BABA GOES TO THE LIBRARY

"Ba-BAH!"

Joyous, he's named me—a first!—from his low crib,
standing in diaper. I've slipped into my daughter's Brooklyn
apartment at seven am, after driving two hours from
Pennsylvania—like every Wednesday for the past year-and-
a-half.

I'm the babysitter.

"Hi, dad," over her shoulder, Sarah at the crib greets me.

I'm locked into the baby's gaze, but somehow, I look
from him to her warm face. She was the baby so recently,
and now she's the mother. I've turned into my own
grandfather.

But—it's my great-grandfather I see in the baby. At the
screen door, giant rectangle face even with mine. "Where's
your father?" he asks. Curly nose-hairs, one sunken eye. Is
this my earliest memory? I know he died just after I turned
four.

How long will my own life overlap my grandson's?

I used to ponder this about my baby son, Sam: of course
he'd long outlive me. Chain-smoking on the back porch at

midnight I'd force myself to stop by murmuring, "Don't kill Sam's dad."

Instead, he died fifteen years ago, aged twenty-three.

"Ba-BAH!" I move into the bedroom and kneel beside Sarah. She slips away; I reach in and lift the baby to a cushion by the window. He scrambles to the closet. Inside are shelves with books. I sing a bouncy melody, "What book will we read today? What book will we read? We will read a book today, what book will we read?" He's pulled *Brown Bear, Brown Bear, What Do You See?* and clambered into my lap. As he flips pages and declares, "Cat! Dog! Horse!"... I'm kneeling at a bottom bookshelf in Eric Carle's Northampton art studio, examining a battered volume bristling with post-it notes. It's a century-old German dictionary, printed in Gothic type. The other Eric Carle Museum staffers are chatting by Eric's drawing desk, but I've fallen into another world. This dictionary's definitions have tiny woodblock illustrations—there must be a thousand of them. Eric's post-its mark animal after animal. These half-inch-high block-print images look just like his famous pictures for *Brown Bear, Brown Bear* and all those other books of his starring angular animals.

I've found his reference.

"Ba-BAH!"

Three hours later, bundled in the green snow coat I inherited when my dad died, I'm pushing my grandson, in his own snow coat and strapped in his stroller, through a brisk February wind down Cortelyou Road. We join a dozen neighbors awaiting the ten am opening of the Cortelyou branch of Brooklyn Public Library. When the smiling librarian approaches the glass door from the inside, and unlocks, we eagerly crowd into the warm, welcoming space.

For years, I commuted to this neighborhood from my home in Amherst, Massachusetts, where I managed The Eric Carle Museum Bookstore. In the process of publishing *Rebel Bookseller,* I'd co-founded the Vox Pop bookstore-café in Brooklyn, and I came in on Wednesdays to present story hours. In all my hundreds of trips between 2004 and 2010, I never even thought of entering this library right down the block from Vox Pop. Why would I? Such a branch does not have the grandeur, prestige and huge inventory of a downtown library.

But now that I'm caring for a baby? I'm absolutely dependent on it. I bring him every Wednesday, and sometimes twice the same day. He and I are acquainted with several neighborhood toddlers and their caregivers, who are also regulars. I can't imagine raising my grandson without this generous, solid, calming library.

I unstrap him from the stroller and pull off his snow coat. He wriggles to the ground and runs unsteadily through the wheeled central bookcases to the children's area. Its large blue rug has a bin of building toys and vehicles set out, and my grandson is now engaged in assembling interlocking blocks. Other toddlers and preschoolers are part of this process as well; we caregivers try to stay back, but we periodically need to intervene to ensure sharing proceeds smoothly.

I'm sitting on the floor, leaning against the tightly packed, spine-out picture-book shelves that line the wall. My grandson comes over, seizes a colorful book and yanks it free. As it emerges, I catch the book and read him its title.

We look at the cover, and I try to get him interested in reading it. But he has grabbed another spine and wrestled the book free of the shelf. Then another. Quickly, he's created a pile of ten books.

I've been trying to interest him in any of these, and he does accept one, and sits in my lap.

We're "reading"—mostly I'm turning the pages quickly and pointing to any image he might recognize: "Do you see the cat?"

It fascinates me that none of his random selections from the shelves of this library are books I stock in my bookstore: they're not "classics" or "standards" or "bestsellers." Rather, they're nearly all recent publications, and "diverse"— meaning, they feature non-white families and individuals. Some are translated into English: originally published in other countries. Others are in Spanish, or Hebrew, or a language of the Indian subcontinent.

I know why, of course, after all I once helped run a bookstore down the street. When we opened Vox Pop in 2004, we trumpeted the fact that we were located in what was called the Most Diverse Census Tract in the United States. This is an "everyone" neighborhood. So, the people who acquired books for this branch library were doing their job, developing a collection where every family living nearby would find books affirming and celebrating their very various lives.

Am I upset that my white grandson finds so many "non-white" books in his local library? Quite the contrary: I want him to encounter the full range of human experience in books.

My own children, in the early 90's, in Chicago were
fortunate to be accepted into an anti-bias daycare center
operated by B.J. Richards. Her extensive collection of
picture books was the cornerstone of her practice. Yes, back
then, thirty-five years ago, there were already hundreds of
"multicultural" books available.

I really have to go back as far as my own childhood, in
the mid-60's, to arrive at a time when it wasn't so. When
Ezra Jack Keats's *The Snowy Day* won the 1963 Caldecott
Medal, it was a landmark event because for the first time
this prestigious award was going to a book with a Black
protagonist. (The author, however, was not Black, a fact
controversial ever since the book's publication.) Keats was
joined by other creators of Black books during the 60's,
including novelists Walter Dean Myers and Virginia
Hamilton, and illustrators Ashley Bryan and Jerry Pinkney.
But the key breakthrough was nineteen-year-old
artist/author John Steptoe's 1969 book *Stevie*—a deeply
emotional, upsetting tale that didn't pull its punches about
its hero's distressed frame of mind.

I met John Steptoe at the 1985 American Booksellers
Association convention in San Francisco. He was thirty-five
then, and I was twenty-five. Watching him sign stacks of his
books in the middle of the crowded Moscone Center was
shocking—because only at that moment did I realize every
other attendee I could see among the thousands of
publishing professionals was white.

I could not imagine how he must have felt.

John Steptoe's thrilling *Mufaro's Beautiful Daughters*
won the Caldecott Honor Award in 1988. He died of AIDS
the next year.

In 1991, the American Booksellers Association launched the American Booksellers Foundation for Free Expression: the ABA had decided that the major challenge facing bookstores was book-banning. Looking back on that moment, I'm astonished. Here we are today, in the midst of a book-banning upsurge. It's so easy to forget that this has been a severe problem for many years. But what's truly remarkable is that pioneers like John Steptoe, who created honest books about the Black child's personal experiences, have in the meantime been victorious: their example has inspired thousands of authors, and validated the actions of lots of publishers and tens-of-thousands of librarians and teachers. In the face of persistent book-banning and censorship, huge numbers of "diverse" books have been created and distributed.

And that's why my grandson sees so many in his library. As the folks at Madison, Wisconsin's Cooperative Children's Book Center—who've been compiling data on the subject since 1985—wrote in *The Horn Book Magazine*:

> The past decade has seen a significant increase in the number and percentage of diverse books published for children and teens, and the number of diverse book creators. This is something to celebrate, and it is a direct result of the greater visibility of activists and advocates in many fields that intersect with children's and young adult literature, whether on social media or in journal articles, the mainstream media, or elsewhere. Their work is part of a movement and a call that stretches back decades, and like many of the voices speaking today, those earlier activists (librarians, educators, critics, scholars, creators, and others) weren't just asking for

more, they were asking for better: better books, with authentic voices and authentic representation....

At the same time, it's impossible to talk about diverse books today without also talking about the fact that they are coming under attack; they are the focus of censorship attempts across the country....

We believe these two things are absolutely connected. When someone walks into a library or classroom today, those spaces look different than in the past. The welcome increase in the number of diverse books has resulted in their greater visibility in libraries and classrooms, and in the lives of children and teens. That visibility is something to celebrate. Unfortunately, it has also made many books targets — flashpoints in the social and political conflicts of our times, without consideration for the children and teens they're intended to reach.

This is especially true of books about LGBTQIA+ and BIPOC lives and experiences, as well as of books that acknowledge how the racism in our nation's present is connected to our nation's past; in other words, books that affirm the lives and realities of children and teens today, including those who are among the most vulnerable in our communities.

My point is simply that our triumph has been in getting so many "diverse" books into print. It didn't happen by itself. Many people had to persist to achieve this objective. Our efforts will continue.

Brown Bear, Brown Bear, What Do You See? contains a hidden symbol: the Blue Horse. This wrong-colored creature is a reference to Eric Carle's experience as a young teen studying art in Nazi Germany. In an era when German Expressionism was banned by the government, because of its nonrealistic style, Eric's teacher, Herr Krauss, was a secret Socialist. As Eric told children's literature historian Leonard S. Marcus,

> *EC:* Herr Krauss...must have been a pretty Bohemian-intellectual-artist type in his youth...he asked me one day to come to his house, where he showed me reproductions of Expressionist and abstract paintings. That was when he pointed out the loose and sketchy quality of my own work, and when I heard him call the Nazis 'charlatans' and *'Schweine,'* which was utterly amazing—a very dangerous thing for him to do.

> *LSM:* Would you say he risked his life by inviting you over?

> *EC:* I certainly think so. As a Socialist and an Expressionist, he already had two strikes against him. If I had turned him in, something I didn't even think of, he would have been interviewed by some horrible official person, who would have brought out his past, his mistakes, and the next thing you know he might have been sent to a concentration camp.

Not long after, Eric encountered the unrealistically-colored work of 1910's artist Franz Marc, co-founder with Wassily Kandinsky of the *Blaue Reiter* movement—also banned by the Nazis. Franz Marc emerged as a major inspiration to Eric.

When Carle created his Blue Horse for the *Brown Bear* book, in New York, twenty-five years later in 1967, he was deploying a personal anti-Nazi image. In 2011, Eric publicly acknowledged his debt to Franz Marc—and to Herr Krauss—with the picture book, *The Artist Who Painted a Blue Horse*. Even in the darkest eras of censorship, the brave actions of individuals make a difference for readers and writers of the future.

My grandson sees a Blue Horse looking at him.

YOU'RE TELLING MY KIDS THEY CAN'T READ THIS BOOK?

2-PUBLISHERS FIGHT: GIVE THE READERS WHAT THEY WANT

The joke goes, "How do you make a small fortune in the book business? Start with a large one." But what if unserved readers present a money-making opportunity? Should book-banners be permitted to keep authors from making money, by keeping readers from books?

"We wrote these for you," American Girl cofounder Valerie Tripp answers her nine-year-old questioner. The bright-eyed child jumps with surprise. Her question—"Who were you thinking of when you wrote the *Felicity* books?"—might have drawn a historical response, since Felicity is a girl of Colonial Williamsburg. But Valerie Tripp, who is moving among the fifty girls in attendance, taking questions, has embraced the chance to make a personal connection. "When I'm writing, I keep you in my mind. I want you to love Felicity."

"I do! I love her so much!" the girl declares.

I'm in Charlottesville at the May 2012 Virginia Festival of the Book. Yesterday, I had my own presentation promoting *Rebel Bookseller,* today I'm the moderator for this panel, "Writing for Boys, Writing for Girls." Like the young American Girl fans, I'm fascinated by Valerie Tripp's tales of the early planning for the American Girl company.

Thirty years before, Valerie Tripp and co-founder Pleasant Rowland had been editors for the textbook company Addison-Wesley. Textbooks depict history in a way that satisfies government committees. Texas has a huge budget and wields disproportionate power over what information gets into textbooks which the entire nation ends up reading. What Texas wants is upbeat, patriotic narrative. Historical episodes that call into question the essential goodness and rightness of the American story must be downplayed or excluded for textbooks to sell in Texas.

Valerie Tripp and Pleasant Rowland had developed an agenda of their own: they wanted to get girls interested in history. Pleasant had the inspiration to launch an upscale historical-doll company that would publish a series of books telling each doll's story. The plan was to pick transformative moments in history and develop thematically matching character-arcs. The American Girls would have personal agency and make hard decisions, so the history lessons would feel personal.

For Valerie and Pleasant to bet on girl-centered historical fiction, in the early 1980's, was audacious. In children's publishing there was a rule-of-thumb: boys won't read books about girls, but girls will read books about boys. So, the need to maximize profit meant every book should star a boy.

Between its 1985 founding and its sale to the Mattel toy company in 2003 for $700 million, American Girl became wildly successful, selling millions of books and roundly disproving the "boy star" rule.

In taking the girl's-eye-view of history, American Girl books provided opportunities for characters to make moral choices and use critical judgement. Some series—like the books about Addy, who starts out enslaved but escapes to freedom—tackled very harsh themes. In October of 1993, my store in Chicago—The Children's Bookstore—hosted the *Addy* books' author, Connie Porter, who is Black. Over four-hundred people came; some drove from hours away. These were mostly white families embracing the chance to raise their daughters' awareness of the travails and hopes of a Black character. Launching a Black doll, Addy, would seem to be a risky choice for a company with a largely white clientele, but American Girl didn't see it that way; their confident marketing director told us the company planned to sell a million *Addy* books the first year alone.

Things seem to have changed in America. On the day of our panel discussion during the 2012 Virginia Festival of the Book, neither Valerie Tripp nor I could have anticipated that a dozen years in our future American Girl books would face parent challenges in Virginia schools and libraries, and that many American Girl books would be banned from schools in Florida. According to a 2023 blogpost on the American Girl website,

> A lot of books dealing with historical and social issues are being banned from Florida schools. These, according to sources from teachers on Twitter and TikTok, include the American Girl historical series with the exception of Felicity and Molly. These bans run the gamut from discussions of slavery in Addy's books to even discussions of anti-Italian xenophobia and polio in Maryellen's books. Yeah... it's *bad*.

The American Girl heroines' change-oriented engagement with the injustices of their eras had become too progressive for book-banning parents of the 2020's.

Maybe it's time for American Girl to launch a doll who fights book-banning.

***

"I feel like I'm looking at the United Nations right now!" author Wade Hudson tells the three-hundred schoolchildren filling the March Elementary School auditorium. This public school a few blocks from Easton, Pennsylvania's Lafayette College indeed has a highly diverse student body. But Wade's comment referred to my introduction of him to the children. I'd told them that just last week, I'd been together with Wade and Cheryl Hudson across the street from the United Nations buildings in New York City. I was the bookseller for the Jane Addams Peace Association's Children's Book Awards ceremony, and Wade and Cheryl had been the honored recipients, for their newest book, *We Rise, We Resist, We Raise Our Voices*. The creation of this anthology of art and writing by fifty outstanding authors had been inspired by the Hudsons' wish to respond to their seven-year-old grandniece's anxiety on learning who had won the 2016 presidential election. To the March students, Wade Hudson then read aloud his poem which opens the book:

> What shall we tell you when our world sometimes seems dark and uninviting?
> What shall we tell you when hateful words that wound and bully are thrown like bricks against a wall, shattering into debris?

What shall we tell you when respect for others and treating others as we wish to be treated appear as yesterday's borrowed wish?...

We shall tell you that love, like cream in milk, will rise to the top and hatred and distrust will be revealed as imposters.

I'd brought Wade Hudson and Cheryl Willis Hudson to Easton as presenters at the Easton Book Festival. Our store, Book and Puppet Company, had launched this festival in 2019 in an effort to reach out to the community with literary programs. We brought authors into all seven Easton elementary schools and four preschools and ran two days of public author programs featuring two-hundred authors. Many authors I recruited were people I'd met over the previous thirty-five years.

The first time I'd hosted Wade and Cheryl was in 1988, at The Children's Bookstore in Chicago. They'd launched a small press called Just Us Books, and were touring nationally to promote their first title, *Afro-Bets ABC Book,* a charming picture book created by Cheryl, starring alphabet letters composed of the twisting bodies of Black children. Between 1988 and 2019, Just Us had published more than seventy books, and sold millions of copies. Wade and Cheryl had also created books published with major publishers like Scholastic; *We Rise, We Resist, We Raise Our Voices* had been published by editor Phoebe Yeh of Crown Books for Young Readers, an imprint of Random House.

The Hudsons had launched Just Us because they couldn't find enough books depicting Black characters, for reading to their own children. Cheryl had worked for a decade in the art departments of the textbook divisions of

Houghton Mifflin and Macmillan publishers. Like the founders of American Girl, Cheryl understood the constraints textbook companies faced—and like Valerie Tripp and Pleasant Rowland, Cheryl recognized this meant there was an opportunity for new companies that would serve readers overlooked by these big publishers.

Wade Hudson was an experienced marketer in the music industry. He applied those skills to distributing Cheryl's books. Just Us Books from the outset targeted Black market outlets to reach the Black families major publishers were mostly ignoring.

Importantly, the context for Black-owned publishers, publishing Black authors and artists, creating books featuring Black characters, will always be the hundreds of years in this country when it was illegal for Black people to learn to read at all.

In staking out their own publishing program, Wade and Cheryl developed a kind of freedom of expression which large corporations didn't have. And in the case of *We Rise, We Resist, We Raise Our Voices,* they were able to extend this positioning into a partnership with just such a corporation, Random House, gathering Black authors and artists to build what became an award-winning anthology.

We Rise, We Resist, We Raise Our Voices was most likely rejected for inclusion by certain libraries, but the knowledge that this could happen did not deter its creators or publisher. They understood that there was a large market for a book speaking to families distressed by the current political environment.

Even in a time of guaranteed book-banning, books that are kept out of some schools can sell well. So, it's a great idea for concerned citizens to create books that refute the culture of repression. If meritorious, such books survive their era to speak to future generations.

The tales of American Girl and Just Us Books—the creation of two "identity" publishers in the 1980's, a women's and a Black company—may seem to show the rise of do-gooder publishing. But, although there was motivation around social issues, both these new companies aimed for profit: smart decisions were being made by innovative entrepreneurs.

The white men in executive positions in the 1980's book industry had failed to understand that here was a money-making opportunity. In recent years, the arrival of more diverse decision-makers at the major publishing companies has enabled the unlocking of additional business income and profits. Maybe losing money in the book business isn't a foregone conclusion—even if your books do get banned.

YOU'RE TELLING MY KIDS THEY CAN'T READ THIS BOOK?

3-EDUCATORS FIGHT: WHO'S SAYING WHAT I CAN'T SAY? THE KKK?

"The 1915 film *Birth of a Nation* by D.W. Griffith was the first blockbuster: adjusted for inflation, it was the most successful film of all time," Allie Jane Bruce, librarian at the Bank Street School for Children tells the hundred-and-fifty educators, librarians and parents attending this April 2016 day of censorship-themed "Who Are You to Say?" panel discussions. "It was one of several factors that led directly to the second coming of the Ku Klux Klan. People died because of that movie."

On the overhead screen here in the Bank Street College auditorium there's a terrible movie-still of a lynching.

"The NAACP organized protests and boycotts and they tried to get some theaters not to show the film. They were successful, in some cases. D.W. Griffith took that and used it to paint himself as a victim. He then went on to make this movie, *Intolerance*...essentially saying that he was Jesus Christ. Now, I sat down and watched both films. That's eight hours of my life I'm never gonna get back."

Laughter.

Allie's point was straightforward, and it was not one this mainstream, mostly white liberal audience was comfortable dwelling on: right-wingers and white supremacists weaponize their constitutionally protected free speech to harm our friends and us.

23

Panelist Cheryl Willis Hudson, the co-founder of Just Us Books, made the same point a bit less directly. She recalled, "I had come up from segregated school systems in Virginia...where our teacher, when she got to a certain section of the history book would always say, 'Okay class, you can put it under your seat.' It was about slavery, and the chapters about slavery actually depicted happy slaves. These were books that were designated and selected by the Virginia state committee.... And the point of view was that slavery was sort of all right and most slaves were treated well. But that didn't really sit too well with all of our Black teachers and the principal."

The line between permissible free speech and impermissible hate speech is drawn differently by different speakers and listeners. D.W. Griffith's claims that others were intolerant disarmed many people who found his speech repugnant. Should speech like his be silenced? And should Cheryl's teacher be permitted by the Commonwealth of Virginia to refuse to expose young Cheryl to the mandated textbook? Who is a censor? Is censoring ever the right thing to do?

The American Civil Liberties Union was founded in 1920, emerging from the National Civil Liberties Bureau, created in 1917 to defend pacifists and conscientious objectors during World War One, when antiwar speech was illegal.

Supreme Court Justice Oliver Wendell Holmes, dissenting against the Court majority's support for criminalizing antiwar speech, wrote, "We must remain eternally vigilant not to suppress the expression of opinions that we loathe." This dissent became a guide to free speech advocates and helps explain why for one hundred years the

ACLU has dependably defended the speech of the Ku Klux Klan and other right-wing groups, even though the ACLU is a liberal organization whose supporters nearly all find the KKK's speech abhorrent.

But another less-discussed reason for liberals to engage in principled, "non-hypocritical" defense of white supremacists' freedom of speech is to deflect attacks. Especially during the 1950's Red Scare, liberal organizations like the ACLU and Bank Street College were routinely labeled Communist sympathizers; evenhandedly defending Anticommunist white supremacists' right to free speech helped the ACLU beat back accusations that they themselves were Communists. Librarian Allie Jane Bruce was in her twenties, many of those attending the Bank Street College censorship panels were decades older—I doubt many of us were thinking clearly about how the Red Scare of sixty-five years before was influencing our strongly held stances.

During that day's closing keynote address, Joan Bertin, director of the National Coalition Against Censorship, responded indirectly to Allie Jane Bruce's complaints about D.W. Griffith's use of his freedom of speech to promote white supremacy. Joan—an ACLU-style free-speech absolutist—said, "Freedom of speech is uncomfortable." Allie, in the audience, used the question time to comment back to Joan, "It seems like I made you a little uncomfortable."

In subsequent years, Allie might have used the phrase "white privilege" to describe Joan Bertin's willingness to defend all speech, no matter how dangerous it might be to, for instance, Black people. Right-wingers nowadays would probably accuse Allie not of being Communist, but being woke.

Freedom of speech has been a battleground for centuries. Bank Street's censorship discussions focused on children's books. Among the dozen panelists were *And Tango Makes Three* authors Justin Richardson and Peter Parnell, whose editor David Gale explained how ten years earlier, in 2006, the book's sales had boomed after tales of its banning went national. Some other panelists were Robie Harris, author of the much-banned sex-education book *It's Perfectly Normal,* and Emily Danforth, author of *The Miseducation of Cameron Post*, a young adult novel about a gay teen. Emily told how the bookstore Browseabout Books in Rehoboth Beach, Delaware had supported gay students in pushing back against their high school's ban of *Miseducation.* Ensuing publicity had scalded the high school administration: by the following year, a tiny gay-straight alliance had ballooned to one-hundred-forty-five students!

I was a panelist myself, charged with presenting the bookseller's perspective on book-banning. Since 2012 I'd managed Bank Street Bookstore; in 2015 I'd moved us to a new location, cutting our rent in half. I told the audience anecdotes to show that modern book-banning weaponizes book-industry practices; this is possible because a few big corporations control much of the market. Independent bookstores play a critical role in fighting book-banning, so their survival is important. The group had already heard Emily Danforth's tale of Browseabout Books; they understood that since independent bookstores operate free of institutional oversight, we participate relatively unimpeded in social battles.

Nothing I said could have outshone the simple fact of my continued presence at Bank Street College: since eight years before my hiring, several powerful trustees had been trying to close Bank Street Bookstore, arguing the college could not continue to subsidize the money-losing operation of a bookstore the bulk of whose clientele was not the Bank Street community, but rather New York City public school educators and Upper West Side families.

My victory was short-lived. I was pressured out in 2017; the bookstore was closed down during the 2020 COVID-19 pandemic.

***

AT THE BOOKSTORE, AN EXCITING PATH AHEAD
Bank Street College website frontpage, June 8, 2012

Six weeks ago, I inherited management of the Bank Street Bookstore from my esteemed colleague Beth Puffer. During her decades of service, Beth placed millions of children's books into the hands of young readers, and myriad professional books into the hands of teachers. Meanwhile, since 1985, I had been selling books at my own stores: The Children's Bookstore and Chicago Children's Museum Store in Chicago, and The Eric Carle Museum Bookstore in Amherst. When the chance came for me to step into Beth's shoes, I was excited and nervous. The bookstore she had developed for Bank Street College was famous worldwide. Could I rise to the challenge?

A challenge it certainly is. This place is busy, and its operations are complex. Over the last few weeks alone, we have:

- Shipped $500 worth of professional education books to a teacher in Copenhagen, and $500 worth to another teacher in Istanbul. Both had selected their books while passing through New York, and for both the visit to Bank Street Bookstore was a long-anticipated event.
- Supplied 60 boxes of books to Ethical Culture School for their spring book fair.
- Hosted 6 first-time authors in a joint publicity event.
- Held a signing with Stephen Colbert for his not-quite-children's-book, *I Am A Pole (And So Can You!)*.
- Built a custom online gift registry to enable anyone to become a donor of LGBT books to New York Public Schools; we're performing this book-supply service as underpinning for the New York City Council LGBT Educational Book Drive.

Meanwhile, all day long parents and children throng the store. Our young customers of course act as if Bank Street Bookstore is a natural part of childhood's landscape, and do not realize how fortunate they are to be growing up near such a resource. Why doesn't every town have a wonderful children's bookstore?

Back in 1989 there were 500 specialty children's bookstores in America; today there are fewer than 100. Bank Street Bookstore survived and grew during the 1990's national collapse in independent bookselling and during this past decade's incredible run-up in Manhattan rents—for one reason only: because the store's parent, Bank Street College, invested in that growth and even stepped in at key junctures to subsidize operating losses.

In similar circumstances, other colleges closed their bookstores or outsourced to national chains, but Bank Street College's leaders understood that the bookstore Beth Puffer was nurturing and growing on their behalf had become a world treasure—a cultural landmark—and was being heavily used by a gigantic and devoted constituency. This bookstore carried the Bank Street College mission far and wide and deserved to be given every opportunity to continue that service even in the face of financial challenges.

As the new manager here, a central aspect of my task is to find a way to ensure that Bank Street Bookstore continues to survive and thrive while reducing the financial burden it can sometimes represent for the College. After all, a dollar fed to prop up the Bookstore is a dollar not available for tuition aid to students. And I do believe that this Bookstore can avoid depending on the College for financial help. We're redeveloping our website, launching an aggressive marketing campaign, and extending our store hours: I have great hopes that by making our terrific book collection and outstanding staff of children's literature experts available during hours that are more convenient to the enormous number of busy New York families and tourists, Bank Street Bookstore can garner enough extra business to pay all our own bills.

So tell your friends: Bank Street Bookstore is now open very early and very late, almost every day. Please make us your first choice.

***

April 2012

Releasing me from a hug, Robie Harris said, "If you ever need help, you have to let me know."

We'd met seventeen years before, in 1995 when I'd sold books during her appearances at Chicago Children's Museum and The Erickson Institute. Robie had been touring to support the launch of *It's Perfectly Normal,* her frank, humorous, fully illustrated children's book about sexuality. Now the book was a controversial classic, in its tenth edition: she'd been updating it to keep pace with shifting ideas among child development specialists.

I'd been alerted by Vice President John Borden to expect support from the Harris Family. The previous fall, when Bank Street College President Elizabeth Dickey had announced the likely closing of the bookstore due to its persistent financial losses, among the loudest voices in protest were Robie Harris's son and daughter-in-law, whose three kids were enrolled in the School for Children.

Robie had studied and taught at Bank Street beginning in the 1960's. She'd collaborated with Irma Black in writing the popular *Bank Street Readers,* which first introduced ethnically diverse characters into reading textbooks. Later, Robie was a stalwart of the Bank Street Writers Lab: she'd had a dozen books published.

Bank Street College of Education—originally the Bureau of Educational Experiments—had been founded as a progressive preschool in 1916 by Lucy Sprague Mitchell, inspired by the writings of philosopher John Dewey. In 1921, having added a teacher-training program, Mitchell launched a Here and Now Movement in children's literature, publishing the *Here and Now Storybook*. Her movement's breakthrough came fifteen years later, when Lucy assigned one of her Bank Street College graduate students, Margaret Wise Brown, the job of creating and editing more Here and Now books, in the context of a new Bank Street Writers Lab. Over the next fifteen years, Margaret Wise Brown's work yielded hundreds of books, including many Little Golden Books that are still popular, and dozens of books Margaret wrote herself, such as *Runaway Bunny* and *Goodnight Moon*. Members of the Bank Street Writers Lab in the 1940's and 1950's included Crockett Johnson *(Harold and the Purple Crayon)*, Ruth Krauss *(The Carrot Seed)*, and Maurice Sendak *(Where the Wild Things Are)*.

Writers Lab member Robie Harris conceived *It's Perfectly Normal* after decades of experience teaching and writing at Bank Street. At Robie's 2024 memorial, her longtime collaborator, illustrator Michael Emberley, told us what it was like during the creation of *It's Perfectly Normal*. He'd spent many days at Robie's kitchen table: "She knew exactly what pictures she wanted. I asked myself, 'Is this the end of my career? Will I ever work after this book?'" Showing naked children—even though they were cartoons—was almost never done in children's books. Robie however, as she'd explained during her April 2016 Bank Street censorship panel session, did not feel there was any question children should be talked with straightforwardly. As for the hundreds of times *It's Perfectly Normal* had been banned, Robie narrated several frustrating episodes, then author Justin Richardson said he'd heard that the most dramatic incident was in Singapore, when a copy had been publicly pulped. Robie threw up her hands—then shrugged.

In the years since the 2016 Bank Street censorship discussions, arguments have continued over whose speech is getting suppressed, progressive liberals' or white supremacists'. Also continuing has been the argument among liberals and progressives about whether—for example—the American Civil Liberties Union should defend the Ku Klux Klan's speech. What hasn't changed is the ongoing publication of more and more innovative, challenging, provocative children's books. Whether every book is available in every library is a shifting situation. But the books exist, they are for sale. They make their way and send their message. That's something Robie Harris fought for.

4-AUTHORS FIGHT: WHY IS *LITTLE BLACK SAMBO* BANNED?

This is often the child's first hero tale, and what a satisfying hero Sambo is! His parents give him wonderful clothes to wear; he loses them to ferocious tigers, but he isn't downed. He uses his wits, rescues his clothes, and turns the silly tigers to good use. No wonder small children love Sambo. He is just the kind of conquering hero they dream of becoming.

—May Hill Arbuthnot, *Children's Books Too Good to Miss,* 1948

An Omaha, Nebraska, barber *[Ernest W. Chambers]* gave graphic testimony to the Kerner Commission's investigation into rioting and unrest among the nation's black population in the late 1960's. Among other remarks, he said:

I sat through *Little Black Sambo*. And since I was the only black face in the room, I became Little Black Sambo. If my parents had taught me bad names to call the little cracker kids—and I use that term on purpose to try to get a message across to you—you don't like it. Well, how do you think we feel when an adult is going to take our child (we teach our child to

respect that adult) and that adult gives these little white kids bad names to call him? Why don't you have Little Cracker Bohunk? Little Cracker Dago? Little Cracker Kike? You can't stand that. But yet you're going to take our little black children and expose them to this kind of ridicule, then not understand why we don't like it.
—Phyllis J. Yuill, "*Little Black Sambo:* A Closer Look. A History of Helen Bannerman's *The Story of Little Black Sambo* and its Popularity/Controversy in the United States," 1976

Let's begin by noticing that *The Story of Little Black Sambo* can easily be purchased on the Internet. Lots of different versions are available, new and used. It can also be read for free, online.

Few bookstores carry *Sambo* on their shelves, and most school and public libraries don't have copies: that decision is made location by location. So, it's true that people who want students to find *Sambo* in their school library have a complaint like those who want to see *And Tango Makes Three* there.

Or is there some other difference between *Sambo* and *Tango*?

Yes. Unlike *And Tango Makes Three*, *Little Black Sambo* has a history as hate speech.

"Sambo" is a racial slur that goes back, via slave-trading, to West Africa in the 1500's. Its technical definition is: a mixed-race Black person who has three Black grandparents and one white grandparent. Since the 1830's, Sambo was the name of one of the stock comedy characters in minstrelsy. Some other regular minstrel men were Tambo, Zip Coon, and Jump Jim Crow. Minstrel shows—which starred whites in blackface dancing and singing, insultingly portraying parodies of Black people—were wildly popular in the United States for one hundred years, from the slavery era until well into the twentieth century. Even the first "talkie" film in 1927, *The Jazz Singer,* starred a minstrel performer: Al Jolson singing "Mammy" in blackface. In *Decolonising Sambo,* Shirley Anne Tate says Sambo is "a stupid Black man but one who is also sly, untrustworthy...the butt of the joke." Joseph Boskin, in *Sambo: The Rise & Demise of an American Jester,* outlines that Sambo appeared in the United States as, "1850s Plantation Darkies...1860s Minstrel Man...1890s-1900s Negro Jokes...1920s Postcard Buffoon...1930s Movie Chauffeur."

Minstrel shows had become successful in England in the 1880's. That's probably when the Scottish youngster Helen Bannerman, living in Edinburgh, encountered minstrelsy.

Helen Bannerman's casual immersion in colonial racial stereotypes was a fact of her life, from her childhood on the island of Madeira off the coast of Africa, to her teen years in Scotland. *Little Black Sambo,* written ten years later in Madras, India—when Bannerman was married to a doctor— was an illustrated letter created to entertain her young children. *Little Black Sambo's* key innovation references familiar children's behavior: the tigers chasing in circles and melting into butter are an emotional translation of a group of children having a passionate argument and wild chase, before subsiding into exhaustion.

Without doubt, the Black characterization in *Little Black Sambo* draws on Helen Bannerman's youthful experience of encountering a minstrel show. (There is, however, zero documentary proof for this.) Some defenders have objected that *Little Black Sambo*—written in India—is really about an Indian child. This does not stand up to careful examination of Bannerman's pictures. In its original version, the book clearly depicts standard blackface-minstrel figures. True, tigers are a staple of Indian folktales, but the Bannerman tigers' focus on eating is universal, like the Troll in "Three Billy Goats Gruff," the Giant in "Jack and the Beanstalk," and the Wolf in "Little Red Riding Hood."

A Black family is the subject of *Little Black Sambo,* but a white woman wrote it, and white people published, sold, read, and loved it. Whenever Black people objected, white people insisted Black people should read and enjoy it.

What's going on?

The book seems to depict a house-servant family. For instance, the mammy—named Mumbo—is pictured as a sort of Aunt Jemima cook. Black servant children were sometimes playmates for the mistress's white children. *Little Black Sambo* may have started out as one white woman's comedic, white-supremacist parable about how Black children, such as Black household playmates, should successfully engage with their naturally subservient, vulnerable situation in life.

But I further speculate that Bannerman's plot derives from an unknown source folktale she heard in childhood, on Madeira, which I will call "Anansi and the Demons": a wily trickster delicately stokes jealousy among his powerful adversaries, brilliantly inciting them through flattery to destroy one another. The Bannerman version of this West African tale represses Trickster's foresighted, scheming agency. Nevertheless, readers of her *Little Black Sambo* do sense Trickster's ineradicable, subversive power.

The thrill of Bannerman's book, for white readers, is unconsciously located in a feeling of uncanny horror that Black people will successfully rise in revolt, as in the Haitian revolution. For some Black readers, an equal but opposite hope and lesson emerges, irrepressible, from the underlying African source: oppressors can be—very carefully—goaded to mutually self-destruct, hoist with their own petards.

***

In 1899, Helen Bannerman's manuscript was brought by a friend from Madras to London, where it was published. Bannerman was paid a few pounds for the copyright; she never received royalties. Unexpectedly, Bannerman's book immediately went into multiple printings. It sold even faster a year later upon its 1900 publication in the United States. Why? Sambo was a minstrel stereotype: the existing popularity of minstrelsy was the basis for the success of *Little Black Sambo* with the white public. Also, since the copyright was not properly controlled, anyone could try making money by publishing their own edition. That's why there was an explosion of versions with egregiously racist pictures: clearly, these horrifying images sold best.

In that Jim Crow era, lynching as a form of entertainment was a common practice. When Black people were about to be lynched, prior to the murder, the enthusiastic mob often demanded the victim dance like a minstrel performer. Whether the victim complied or no, he would be strung up on a tree. Dying of strangulation, his legs would twitch wildly. The lynch mob would laugh at this "dancing." This is why—no matter that Helen Bannerman lived in India when she wrote her story, no matter that she wrote for her children—when *The Story of Little Black Sambo* was published in the United States, it became hate speech. The clownish Sambo—that well-known minstrel dancer—is always destined for humiliation and possible death.

Little Black Sambo himself does not die in his book for one reason: folkloric animals are not as smart as white humans. Folkloric animals are stupider even than the lowly Sambo! The foolish tigers, like small children, forget what they ought naturally to do, which is to both exploit and eat Sambo. Instead, these tigers fight amongst themselves. Thus, Sambo survives to gorge on tiger-butter.

The moral of the book—for white people—is, don't act like a stupid animal and get thrown off by what Sambo says or does. Don't be distracted by your jealousy of what other white people have. Eat or be eaten! Let's all enjoy ourselves together by stealing Sambo's culture and killing Sambo.

Little Black Sambo retains its character as hate speech. In the recent past, it was inciting readers to join a lynch mob. Today, it still teaches white children to work together bullying Black children.

It teaches Black children—as a surface message—that when bullying starts, offer to be exploited, give in. That's your only chance. Hey, it worked for Little Black Sambo!

***

When I was on the 2016 Bank Street College censorship panel with Cheryl Willis Hudson, her slideshow included horrible *Sambo* illustrations. She said that as a kid, it was the only book she saw with Black characters, and the book hurt her.

Of course, I thought of earlier times I'd heard those words: "*Little Black Sambo* hurt me."

When it comes to fighting "bad" speech, Supreme Court Justice Louis Brandeis wrote in 1927, "If there be time to expose through discussion the falsehood and fallacies, to avert the evil by the processes of education, the remedy to be applied is more speech, not enforced silence." I am fortunate to have been friends with a man who carried out a brilliant "more speech" response to his being hurt as a child by *Little Black Sambo*.

One afternoon, in early 2003, I was standing at The Eric Carle Museum Bookstore cash register when Jerry Pinkney stopped in. He'd been attending a museum board meeting: he was a founding trustee. Jerry had published dozens of picture books and won almost every award. Jerry asked, "Andy, do you have a copy of this year's Caldecott Medal winner?" I zipped to the shelf and returned with Eric Rohmann's *My Friend Rabbit*. Jerry paged through and murmured, "A wordless book." He looked up.

"That's true," I said, "It does seem unusual they'd pick a wordless book for the Caldecott." I knew that Jerry Pinkney, the most famous and successful Black children's book author/illustrator, had won several Caldecott Honor Awards, the runner-up prize—including that year's, for *Noah's Ark*. But neither Jerry Pinkney nor any Black person had, in its seventy-year history, won the Caldecott Medal itself.

"What do you think of this book?" Jerry asked.

"I might not have picked it," I answered. "But I have friends who've been on the Caldecott committee. I've heard it can be political. Rumor had it that one year in the late 80's there were two factions. Each hated the other group's favorite. They settled on giving the Medal to a book nobody thought was best. The books people really liked got Honor Awards."

Jerry set the book down and looked at me.

I said, "So, Jerry—can I tell you a story, and ask you a question?"

He smiled and glanced out the picture window towards the parking lot. I knew he needed to drive two hours to get home. But it wasn't late in the afternoon. "Okay," he answered.

"Jerry," I began, "back in 1989—when I still had The Children's Bookstore—I was on the ABA/CBC Joint Committee. American Booksellers Association and Children's Book Council each supplied five people, so, it was a ten-person thing: five children's booksellers and five children's book publishers. We met twice. Our job was to create a day of programming for booksellers to attend on the Friday before the 1990 ABA Convention."

Jerry said, "You were invited to do that? Pretty fancy, Andy."

"Yeah," I said. "I was thirty. The baby in the room. Well, so, our first meeting, October 1989, in the Children's Book Council offices in Manhattan—there was a break. CBC gave us all lunch in a separate conference room."

Jerry said, "I remember their old offices."

"So, I was sitting eating lunch, next to Valerie Lewis, from Hicklebee's in San Jose."

"Yes, Valerie—she's wonderful."

"And, while we were eating there at the table, David Reuther—from Morrow Junior Books—a committee member from the Children's Book Council side—strolled over to where the booksellers were eating together, and said, 'Can I ask you a question?'"

Jerry said, "Oh, I'm good friends with David. Yes."

"David said, 'Can I just ask you two—do either of you....' And here he kind of stepped back, and paused, and took in the other three booksellers with his glance, and he said, 'Do any of you...sell *Little Black Sambo*?'"

Jerry looked surprised, but said, "Okay, I think I know where you may be going here."

"Valerie said, 'We don't keep it in stock. But we'll get it for someone who special orders it.' I could see that none of the other booksellers were paying attention to this conversation. I answered David, 'I don't always have it, but sometimes I order two copies and let them sell. Then I wait a year and order two more.' David asked, 'Why do you do it that way?'"

"I explained, 'The summer before we opened in 1985, I saw *Little Black Sambo*—the original, small version with the Bannerman pictures—in the Harper catalog. I decided that since we were aiming to open the largest children's bookstore in Chicago, we should be comprehensive. We needed to include *Sambo* in the inventory. I knew it was racist, but also, it was of historical importance. I ordered two.' David seemed interested. Valerie said, 'We don't want customers to see that book in our store.'"

"I said, 'Sure, well, it's a very small book. When we were setting up the store, I never faced it out. For months we didn't sell any. But, one day, I answer the phone and a lady asks, 'Do you have *Little Black Sambo*?' So, I say, 'Yes.' The lady says, 'You have it? You really have it? Do you have it now?' I say, 'Sure.' She says, 'Well, I live a ways away, but I'm getting in my car, and I'll be there in an hour. Will you make sure not to sell it?' I say, 'Okay.' She says, 'Do you know that no other bookstore has it? That was my favorite book growing up, and later I raised my children on it. Now I'm a grandmother. I want to share this wonderful book with my grandchildren, but I cannot find it anywhere!' So, I say, 'Well, I have it. I don't know about anyone else.'"

"An hour later an older North Shore-type white lady with piled-up hairdo rushes through the door. She's gushing—she repeats everything she said on the phone. Very excited to get the book but also simmering with resentment at how hard it was for her."

Jerry said, "Okay."

"So, I say to David and Valerie, 'My story isn't finished. The book must have sold to someone else, a few months later, because I realized that we'd sold out. I bought two more copies. Again, they sat on the shelf, for months, spine out. Then one day, a well-dressed, middle-aged Black lady approaches me while I'm shelving books, thrusts *Little Black Sambo* at me, and asks, 'What is this book doing in this store? I have always appreciated your selection of books for all customers. I would never have expected to see this book, here, of all places. You need to know that *Little Black Sambo* hurt me. It hurt me, as a child, personally. I have always loved this store, but I assure you, you will never see me again.' She placed the book down and walked towards the door. When she reached it, she turned and said, 'I will be telling my friends.'"

Jerry said, "She did tell you!"

"Yeah, that's when I first realized how super-weird it was that this book with Black characters was only used by white people. So, then David says, 'Let me stop you, Andy. I asked if you were carrying *Sambo* for a reason.'"

Jerry said, "Here we come to why you wanted to talk with me!"

I said, "Sorry I made you listen to all that, but yes. David says, 'Jerry Pinkney wants to illustrate *Little Black Sambo* and he's asking if we'll publish it. I wonder if you would sell it.'"

Jerry said, "David Reuther polled you! Is that something editors do with booksellers before publishing a book?" I said, "Not with me. Maybe they ask Barnes and Noble. I guess he was just taking advantage of the moment." Jerry asked, "What did you tell him? You're the one who was selling the original."

"Well, so, Valerie said, 'We would normally sell anything by Jerry Pinkney. But the staff would have to decide as a group to carry that one.' I said, 'I agree, I would pick it up if it was Jerry Pinkney. So, why does he want to do it?' Valerie echoed, 'Yes, David, why does he want to?' David said, 'He's been working on it for years. He has an idea he could change things, repair something.' Valerie said, 'If he can do that, I'm all for it.'"

Jerry said, "Well, David Reuther didn't take that book."

"In 1996, when *Sam and the Tigers* came out, of course I saw it was Dial and not Morrow, and Julius Lester was the author. So—I just wondered, what was the story there? I guess it took me a long time to get around to my question!"

Jerry said, "No, it's fine. That was interesting. And your customer who told you the book hurt her, that was me. But I'd loved the Bannerman original; it was the racist rewrites that hurt me. Years later, when I saw Charles Blockson's Afro-American Collection at Temple University, including fifty racist versions, I realized I needed to set things right by creating a sympathetic, positive *Sambo*. David Reuther wasn't the only editor who turned me down. By the 80's, nobody wanted to get into hot water by publishing a new *Sambo*."

"So, how did you get Dial to do it?"

"The breakthrough was when Julius joined me on the project. Together, we were able to land a deal with Phyllis Fogelman. Dial had already done well with our adaptation of Br'er Rabbit."

"Well, I stopped carrying *Sambo* in 1989, after that Children's Book Council conversation, but I was glad to be able to start carrying your *Sam and the Tigers,* in 1996."

In 2010, seven years after our conversation, Jerry Pinkney became the first Black person to win a Caldecott Medal, with the wordless book *The Lion & the Mouse*. Like *Little Black Sambo* and *Sam and the Tigers, The Lion & the Mouse* is a tale in which a big cat menaces a weaker character. Unlike with *Sambo* and *Sam,* though, cat and prey both survive to benefit from the happy ending.

***

Jerry Pinkney and Julius Lester have passed away. For thirty years, *Sam and the Tigers* has provided generations of children with not just a marvelous storybook, but also— when needed—a tool to assist families and educators with "compare and contrast," helping children cope with the unavoidable existence of the variously racist versions of *Little Black Sambo.*

Here's a brief comparison of *Sam and the Tigers* and *Little Black Sambo,* to show some story-elements Julius Lester and Jerry Pinkney must have thought made *Sambo* problematic for Black families.

1) *Sam and the Tigers:* All characters' names are the same: "Sam." So, it's who you are inside, as a person, that matters.
   What was wrong with *Little Black Sambo*? One hundred years of children enduring nasty name-calling.

2) *Sam and the Tigers*: Sam chooses his own brightly colored clothes, sometimes over the objection of his concerned parents. He visits shops in his neighborhood staffed by friendly animals.
   What was wrong with *Little Black Sambo*? Lack of decision-making agency for Sambo, parental unconcern with Sambo's welfare wearing fancy clothes in the jungle, absence of community, social isolation for the family.

3) *Sam and the Tigers: Sam* is enthusiastically on his way to school.
   What was wrong with *Little Black Sambo*? Lack of purpose for Sambo's risky walk through the jungle.

4) *Sam and the Tigers:* Sam has nuanced, intelligent interactions with the tigers. They are known threats to whom he must relate cautiously.

What was wrong with *Little Black Sambo*? The hapless, strangely "lucky" way Sambo avoids getting eaten, even though he must have had some familiarity with bribery, or "paying protection." (Sambo's inexplicable lack of wily, foresighted intention in these pivotal moments is for me evidence that Helen Bannerman repressed her character's original African identity as a folkloric Trickster like Anansi, full of agency and crafty flattery.)

5) *Sam and the Tigers:* Sam invites the community of animal shopkeepers to his family's hearty meal of pancakes. The group calmly notes that tigers in their neighborhood have vanished. Since we know Sam is responsible for this, we realize Sam has helped his community.
What was wrong with *Little Black Sambo*? Sam's family showed no generosity to others when they had excess food. Nobody else was helped by Sambo's actions.

I do not know if the inclusion of *Sam and the Tigers* in school libraries has been challenged, but I do think it's a wonderfully helpful book.

5-LIBRARIANS FIGHT: GUARD TRADITION OR GUIDE GROWTH?

If people didn't fuck, you wouldn't have any children, and without children you would be out of work!
—Tomi Ungerer, bestselling picture-book author, at the 1969 American Library Association convention, shouting at a roomful of children's librarians who were collectively berating him for having published his book of adult sex-satire cartoons, *Fornicon*.

[Tomi Ungerer's] punishment was to be effectively blacklisted in America, his books taken from libraries, his children's publishing career in America over.
—Robert Sullivan, "Tomi Ungerer's Triumphant Return," *New Yorker,* 2015

Children's librarians today are on the front lines, working against book bans. Modern librarianship has a punk aesthetic: pink hair, tattoos and a nose ring.

This wasn't always so.

For much of the twentieth century, librarians were stereotyped as strait-laced, glasses-wearing, buttoned-up, asexual women, their hair in a tight bun, whose notorious habit was aggressively shushing library patrons. For instance, in the popular 1957 musical, *The Music Man,* con-man Harold Hill takes it for granted that Marian, the "Madam Librarian," must be such a person.

Children's rooms in libraries, pioneered by New York City chief children's librarian Anne Carroll Moore, were created—in part—to keep kids away from the "inappropriate" literature written for adults.

That aspect of the rooms' mission was censorship.

In the case of Tomi Ungerer, this uptight mission extended to including in children's-book evaluation a consideration of an author's other books, written for adults.

Back in the 60's, most parents didn't buy books for their children; the library was how families obtained books. Publishers relied on librarian spending-power and paid close attention to what sorts of books librarians wanted. Thus, librarians had influence over not just readers, but also publishers: librarians were instrumental in the development of the "walled garden" of children's literature, as a genre.

That's why libraries were the way they were when I was a kid. For instance, nowadays, the children's biography section is filled with stories of rebels and resisters and brave individuals who dared to be different. But back then, the biography section was epitomized by *Childhood of Famous Americans,* a series of somewhat fictionalized patriotic hagiographies, meant, I suppose, to teach that future greatness will reveal itself in youth.

That's how librarians wanted it. They were guardians of tradition.

Librarians acted both individually and collectively to shape the actions of publishers. The American Library

Association and many regional and specialty groups created recommended-book lists and thematic book awards, to guide librarians in collection development. Publishers struggled to understand exactly what criteria librarians were using, to publish books that librarians would buy.

The battles a century ago inside the children's book world seem peculiar. Why did Anne Carroll Moore so strongly dislike Margaret Wise Brown's books, refusing to buy *Goodnight Moon* for the New York Public Library children's room? Because it has no plot!

Why did librarians across the country dislike Maurice Sendak's 1964 Caldecott-Medal-winning *Where the Wild Things Are*? Because Max is disobedient to his mother but ultimately receives no punishment!

Can it be true that librarians ripped out the page in William Steig's 1970 Caldecott-Medal-winning animal fable *Sylvester and the Magic Pebble,* on which policemen are depicted as pigs? Yes—we should not make fun of authority!

This was internecine conflict: some librarians were awarding the Caldecott Medal, others disliked the winning books but were "forced" to buy them, since no library could ignore patron expectations that each year's Medal-winners would be included in local library collections.

Meanwhile, editors like George Nicholson of Dell Publishing had begun sidestepping librarians, releasing already-published hardcover books in paperback, for sale directly to children in the new mall-bookstore chains. That's how Judy Blume's scandalous 1970 *Are You There God? It's Me Margaret* reached girls' hands, not through libraries. But Maurice Sendak's *In the Night Kitchen* was a 1971 Caldecott Honor Award winner, and though many librarians didn't approve of bold three-year-old Mickey's penis appearing in several pictures, they felt obliged to acquire the book because it had won the award. Their recourse was to use an Exacto knife to slice out the offending image, or a white-out brush to paint over it.

The American Library Association pushed back:

> In 1973, the ALA sponsored a petition asking librarians (primarily in Louisiana and Pennsylvania) not to paint diapers on Maurice Sendak's Mickey, the unclothed hero of *In the Night Kitchen*, or to rip out the page in *Sylvester and the Magic Pebble*, a book about a donkey...that features helpful and courteous police officers who are pigs.
> —Robert Sullivan, *New Yorker*, 2015

In 1982, the American Library Association started proactively celebrating Black authorship when it took over administration of the 1969-founded Coretta Scott King Awards. Also in 1982, in a definitive shift away from conservatism, ALA launched Banned Books Week, systematically mobilizing opposition to book-banning.

The relationship between librarians and publishers shifted after 1981 when President Reagan cut federal funding for libraries; this reduction in library buying-power forced children's publishers to try sell more books to families—through bookstores—and to teachers, who had begun spending personal money to create classroom libraries. Families and teachers comprised different kinds of market segments than librarians. These buyers were less organized—a decentralized patchwork. Learning to sell to them required children's publishing companies to undergo further transformation and explore new opportunities.

Still, the American Library Association remained the most forceful voice in the children's literature conversation.

In 1984, when Christine Bluhm and I were developing The Children's Bookstore, we understood little of this, nor did we foresee how opening in Chicago—home to the American Library Association, several library schools, and an excellent public library system—would shape the bookstore.

We launched our children's-literature education by visiting legendary professor Zena Sutherland. Here's how I describe the meeting in *Rebel Bookseller:*

> Unfortunately, we knew practically zilch about children's literature. Working with Child's Play Touring Theatre performing thousands of stories written by children themselves hadn't taught me anything about children's books. Working in a dozen general bookstores had taught Chris *some,* but not enough to competently fill a complete children's bookstore. She started doing research and discovered there was a special library at the University of Chicago associated with their doctoral program in library science, called the Center for Children's Books. This place was operated by someone named Zena Sutherland.
>
> One day in October of '84 Chris and I went down to the University of Chicago library and buzzed the intercom of the Center for Children's Books. We hadn't made an appointment.
>
> Someone answered the intercom. We went up the elevator. A short, fierce-looking sixty-something woman

with blond-white hair admitted us to the Center. She asked why we'd come. We explained we were preparing to open a children's bookstore and hoped to browse this library for ideas about what books to sell.

Zena Sutherland scrutinized us. She began asking questions. I felt like I was back in third grade, but Chris was sturdier. Once Zena had determined that we knew very little about the field of children's literature, she said, "Come into my office."

Seated behind her desk, she announced, "The first thing you should do is read my book."

I asked, "What book?"

Her eyes widened, and she answered, *"Children and Books,"* producing a college textbook and handing it to Chris. It was in its sixth edition. At this point I realized we should have called for an appointment.

Chris was undaunted and started asking questions. I was relieved to see Zena understanding Chris wasn't a novice bookseller. Zena said, "You're going to get a lot of support for this project. Many people have been waiting for this a long time. You should join the Children's Reading Round Table right away. There are fifteen-hundred members—authors, librarians, teachers—they'll want to be involved, and they'll provide good advice and send you business. You may even be able to hire some to work for you. When will you open?"

I was startled by this shift from challenging to welcoming. Perhaps she wasn't a dragon? After we left, Chris said Zena was like her mother.

Again, we did exactly what our expert told us to. We bought Zena's book and worked our way through it. We'd already requested sales catalogs from two-hundred publishers. Over the next several months we compared these publisher lists, author by author, title by title, with the index of *Children and Books*. Flipping back and forth between catalogs and textbook, we taught ourselves children's literature, and in the process compiled the opening order for The Children's Bookstore.

In May of 1985, Chris and I visited Madison, Wisconsin, where we met another leading librarian, Ginny Moore Kruse, again, without having a clear idea of her importance to the field of children's literature. Our visit to the Cooperative Children's Book Center (CCBC) had been suggested by Karen Rizzo, a Children's Reading Round Table-member librarian we'd hired to help us develop our store's collection.

Ginny was friendly and encouraging. During our conversation, she showed us a new CCBC report documenting how many books published the previous year had included a Black character. Less than one percent! Ginny said she planned to collect such statistics annually.

Over the next forty years, CCBC's increasingly detailed analyses benchmarked the children's book industry, guiding creators as they pressed for more wide-ranging representation of characters and situations.

Today's increased diversity in children's books has, in turn, attracted an activist cohort to the profession of library science: booklovers fighting to develop and protect collections whose existence is conceivable only in the context of a publishing transformation that happened during those librarians' own childhoods.

In 2025, the Position Statement of the American Association of School Librarians includes providing:

Diverse and inclusive resources, programs, and services that meet the needs of all learners; represents various points of view on current and historical issues; and provides support across a wide range of interest areas with opportunities for learners to recognize themselves.

In May 2025, the Librarian of Congress, Dr. Carla Hayden, was fired by the president. One of her offenses, according to the White House, was, "putting inappropriate books in the Library for children." However, by law, *every* copyrighted book *must* be collected by the Library of Congress: from *Sambo* to *Tango*. The absurdity of this throwaway explanation for firing the first Black female Librarian of Congress—in the ninth year of her congressionally approved ten-year term—shows that the moral-panic rationale for book-banning is a thinly veiled excuse for racist bullying as a form of popular entertainment, playing to the base: a minstrel tiger prancing in stolen clothes.

In 2018, Roger Sutton, editor of *The Horn Book Magazine,* interviewed Librarian of Congress Carla Hayden. They'd both studied library science under Zena Sutherland in 1980's Chicago. Back then, I reviewed children's books alongside Roger Sutton on Chicago Public Radio, and Carla Hayden brought me into her library at the Museum of Science and Industry to run a science bookfair as part of her community-outreach campaign.

Carla Hayden: Remember when the motto was: Let the books battle it out on the shelves? We had something to offend everyone, and we were proud of that. Yes, we'll put them right there. You decide. That's almost a creed.

Roger Sutton: Libraries present people with the world, basically. All kinds of crazy ideas and smart ideas and ideas I agree with and ideas I loathe.

Carla Hayden: Ideas that worked and didn't work. Ideas from a long time ago, new ideas, all of that. And you get to decide. You get to pick. Think of the freedom that gives you, that you can pick what you want to read. That's the essence of the whole thing.

***

Tomi Ungerer was returning to the United States for the first time in forty years, when he came to The Eric Carle Museum of Picture Book Art in 2010. We'd mounted a full-scale retrospective exhibition. In the museum store, alongside several titles recently released in the US by Phaidon Press, I had on display stacks of Ungerer's books imported from France, Germany, Spain and Switzerland. When Tomi walked into the store, he smiled broadly on seeing dozens of titles released between 1970 and 2010 only in Europe, now for sale in America.

Tomi Ungerer and Eric Carle shared the auditorium stage for a public conversation. Both had suffered in childhood under wartime Nazism. Tomi told Eric he'd first come to the US from Strasbourg in 1956, with fifty-two dollars in his pocket. Eric one-upped Tomi, responding that he'd come to America from Stuttgart in 1952 with forty-two dollars in his pocket.

Today, each author has a museum named after him. Tomi's however is on multiple levels, and while the main floor and upstairs are devoted to children, the downstairs features Tomi's erotica.

Europeans may be a bit more sexually open-minded than Americans.

A dozen of Tomi Ungerer's picture books—and several of his books for adults—are in print in the US. Check our website: I stock them at Book and Puppet Company.

6-PARENTS FIGHT: WE'LL CREATE BOOKS FOR OUR CHILDREN

One day, I took my 3-year-old son, Jojo, to a barber. I explicitly asked the barber not to shave off all of Jojo's hair and to just make it shorter. The barber then proceeded to, in my view, shave Jojo's head practically bald. "Whoa, whoa, I told you that I did not want it bald, this is way too low!" I exclaimed. "How can I tell you this? You've got a real nig*** here. He is a native boy. He is from the tribe. This ain't pretty hair. This is the best cut for him," said the black barber with clippers still in the front of Jojo's hair.

I was sick for days after the incident. The n-word is such a filthy word. I did not know what to do to shield my own sons and all of our children from such manifestations of racism, both internalized and externalized.

A long time ago, I heard someone say that all pain should be turned into art in order to make pain beautiful. But how was I going to make it art? I'm a critical writer, not an artist. But one day I was watching Super Soul Sunday on OWN and a speaker said that art is no different from prayer so I prayed to God for a story. God gave me *Sunne's Gift*.

—Ama Karikari Yawson, *Kickstarter*, 2014

"Excuse me, I wrote a children's book. How should I get it published?" a customer asked.

I had just finished chatting with author Ama Karikari Yawson, who a few minutes before had concluded her Bank Street Bookstore reading of *Sunne's Gift*, an anti-bullying creation myth about the origin of luxuriant hair.

Every day, people ask me how they can publish a book they've written. It's a huge challenge to get your work "conventionally published"—that is, to get a contract from a publishing company for cash advance with royalties, plus editorial, manufacturing, marketing and distribution services. I never want to talk in detail with walk-in authors about how they can attain this difficult objective. My usual advice is that they join the Society of Children's Book Writers and Illustrators (SCBWI). Within this support network, composed of thousands of already-published and not-yet-published writers, they may learn the tried-and-true techniques needed to reach their goal.

Ama Karikari Yawson's book launch had pulled a good crowd—about two dozen. Several were people who had supported the Kickstarter fundraiser she'd run to underwrite her self-publishing effort: she'd raised twelve-thousand dollars to pay her illustrator and print high-quality hardcovers of *Sunne's Gift*.

"Hello? I wrote a children's book. How should I get it published?"

I prepared to launch into my standard riff about joining SCBWI—but Ama intervened. She stepped forward and began to give her own response, before I could give mine. Ama said, "Do a Kickstarter." She quickly unfurled the tale of how she'd written and published *Sunne's Gift*. Ama and the customer exchanged contact information, and the customer left looking empowered and happy.

It used to be called vanity publishing, and for decades I routinely refused to carry self-published books. Why? A laundry list of objections boils down to, "This doesn't look like a professionally published book and no-one's gonna buy it from me."

When I opened The Children's Bookstore in 1985 I learned there were about a million books in print, available to order from publishing companies, and these publishers released about two-hundred-thousand more books every year. Also, ten-thousand vanity-press books came out every year, but I need pay no attention to the vanity press because there were no buyers for those books.

For me, only one number mattered: there were four-thousand quality children's literature titles released every year, from the leading publishing houses. Those were the books I needed to learn about and choose amongst for The Children's Bookstore.

Today, forty years later, there are thirteen million titles I can order from the largest industry wholesaler, Ingram Book Company: perhaps three million are professionally published, and ten million are self-published. This flood of self-publishing is the result of the development of online distribution: nowadays people upload a digital file to a website and call their book published.

Ama Karikari Yawson's crowdsourcing approach is a third way, which often results in a higher-quality self-published book, because there's a real operating budget. Plus, Kickstarter gave Ama a task-flow that resulted in hundreds of advance sales—a great start on marketing and distribution.

No matter how self-published authors do it, their long-term goal usually remains to transition their book to a professionally published stream of distribution and income. They want a "real" publisher. That's because most self-published books don't sell well; the marketing efforts of the big companies reach more readers.

***

My son passed away in 2010. Not long after, I told my daughter I would write a book about him. I had a small collection of his stories and poems I also wanted to publish. But I couldn't start. It was too painful.

A year later, I decided I needed to break out of my comfort zone at The Eric Carle Museum, and I applied to manage Bank Street Bookstore in Manhattan. They hired me, and I inherited a staff of nine full-time booksellers.

I'd decided that the way I could write about my son would be to use the story of the next phase of my life as a frame. Since I was constantly thinking about him, since everything reminded me of him, since I was always in danger of falling into the past, this seemed like a good way to tell his story. At our first staff meeting, I handed each of my new employees a copy of *Rebel Bookseller* and told them, "I'm going to write a book about whatever happens while I'm at Bank Street."

If I thought my plan to include them in my next book might lead the staff to cooperate with my efforts to turn Bank Street Bookstore around, I was mistaken. They didn't like my business strategy, and also, they didn't seem

concerned that I planned to report on their behavior, in my
future opus.

During my five years at Bank Street, I did do some work on
my book, but I was so busy that I couldn't get far. Only after
Rebecca Migdal (now known as Gaia Abraxas) and I had set
up our new store, Book and Puppet Company, in Easton,
Pennsylvania, did I focus on the memoir about my son. I
wrote it quickly.

My *Rebel Bookseller* contract with Seven Stories Press
gave them the right of first refusal. When I'd completed
what I felt was a strong draft for the text that ultimately
became *Son of Rebel Bookseller,* I sent it in. My publisher,
Dan Simon, wrote me back:

> The manuscript is moving, and the attempt to bring
> together the tragedy of your loss and the struggle to save
> the store is admirable and ambitious in the best sense.
> But our feeling is that you still have a very significant
> way to go to fully connect the two themes in a way that
> would make them feel integrated, each informing the
> other in a meaningful way.
>
> I also think there are legal concerns. Even if you
> change people's names and attributes, any one of the
> people involved at the store or from the administration
> at Bank Street College could take offense and threaten to
> sue. I actually think that would be more likely to happen
> if you were published by a known and respected book
> publisher than if you, say, self-published.
>
> Rather than slow you down, I think we really have to
> pass on this. I wish you all the good luck in the world
> with it.

Here was a strange truth: I could not tell the story of what happened at Bank Street because I might get sued for defamation!

A few weeks after receiving Dan's email, I attended a college reunion brunch in New York and found myself in conversation about my problem with a classmate from decades before, who'd had a long career in publishing. She disagreed with Dan Simon, saying that if I was going to release a memoir that might attract a lawsuit, I should use a large publishing house. To illustrate her point, she told me a story. She'd been at Crown Publishing when they released *Primary Colors,* published anonymously. This bestselling *roman a clef* had exposed scandalous stories from inside the 1992 Bill Clinton presidential campaign, using a lightly fictionalized narrative. Crown had expected to be sued, but since they knew the book would be a bestseller, they felt they'd have plenty of funds to settle lawsuits, and still earn a profit.

I asked, "So, did Crown get sued?"

"At first, no. As more and more copies sold, we thought any day, we're going to be sued. But we weren't. A year passed. We figured, wow, no-one sued us! But then, eighteen months later, we were sued."

"Who went after you?"

"The craziest thing. One of the made-up sections in the book had the Hillary Clinton character in a romantic affair with a Black male librarian in Harlem. Well, it turns out, there really is a Black male librarian in Harlem, and one of his friends read the book, and told him he was in it. That's who sued—because, he had not really had an affair with Hillary. We checked with our author: he'd had no idea if

there were or weren't any Black male librarians in Harlem—
he'd made his character up."

"So, did you defend against the lawsuit?"

"We paid thousands of dollars to settle."

"What? But the guy was wrong—he wasn't being
defamed!"

"We'd made a lot of money on the book. It was better to
make the lawsuit go away. But that's why you need to have a
major publishing house: they have lawyers, they budget for
lawsuits. You can't afford that, if you self-publish. Anyone
can sue, even if they don't have a real case."

Unfortunately, I couldn't find any agent or editor to take my
book. I gradually realized that, despite my classmate's
advice, self-publishing was my only option. I joined
Independent Book Publishers Association for support in
doing my project, and they referred me to a specialty
insurance company. I submitted my manuscript and
requested a quote for a million dollars in libel coverage.

Three thousand dollars.

I set the project aside.

I felt stuck. I turned my attention to founding Easton
Book Festival. A year passed.

My dad died. For years, he'd been nagging me to write
another book. I felt like I had to resume my effort.

I'd sent a copy of the manuscript to Mira Bartok—a
friend who'd written the bestselling memoir *The Memory
Palace*—asking for advice. We scheduled a phone call. Mira
surprised me by launching into a critique of the text. She
said, "This can't be a memoir about Bank Street. It has to be
about your son. When I run workshops, I tell writers there
are two kinds of memoirs, little and big. The little memoir is,

'This terrible thing happened to me'—like at a job. The big memoir is morality and mortality."

I understood that I had allowed my anger at Bank Street—the little memoir story—to obscure my true objective, which was to write a book about my son, as I'd promised my daughter. That was the big memoir.

I knew what to cut—I removed half the text—and I knew what to add—lots of short anecdotes about my son, and many brief passages from his journal and papers.

I self-published. I set the book up, not on Amazon, but a competing online print-on-demand platform, Ingram Spark.

Son of Rebel Bookseller has sold only a few hundred copies. But—I finished it; it exists.

I took out the stuff I could have gotten sued for—it wasn't interesting anyway. Job nonsense happens to everyone, right?

But—the fact that I was not allowed to tell my life story because I might get attacked by people about whom I was telling the truth—I do feel that kind of censorship is weird.

Also, it's weird to feel censored by the publishing industry: those endless rejections from agents and editors are exhausting and disheartening.

It used to be that vanity publishing was looked down on. Now it's a free-for-all, and most people do it without feeling ashamed—but most all of us who self-publish have few readers.

It's just that self-publishing feels like our only way forward.

Ama Karikari Yawson's *Sunne's Gift* and my *Son of Rebel Bookseller* were both written by parents who could not take no for an answer.

7-INTERLUDE: CELL VS. SOUL—ON UNDERSTANDING PERSUASION

By Samuel Laties, aged thirteen
From *Son of Rebel Bookseller*

CELL: What would you call living?

SOUL: The inner consciousness of man, which is the soul.

CELL: I must respect your views my friend, but to me it seems that the inner consciousness of man was not given to us by God, but evolved, through trial and error.

SOUL: I am sorry, my friend but I must also respectfully disagree. You see it is, in my view, impossible for this process to have taken place. How could we who have such broad depth of thought, who can contemplate what life is, who can imagine and dream such wondrous things, how can such a being that can perform these actions have come from an ape?

CELL: I can see your line of reasoning, but it is to no avail, for there is no great proof that stands behind your thoughts. All that you say are words of your imagination; evolution is the only possibility that can be shown true. Humans have believed in divine gods and spirits for upwards of ten thousand years. Hundreds of gods have been embraced by tens of millions each. How can your one faith be true when it is only one of hundreds?

SOUL: The soul is a belief of not one faith, but of many, for almost all the people of the world past and present have believed—understood—that body is more than flesh and bone; it is composed of the inner self, which is the soul. How can you presume that billions of people worldwide uniting in one common view can be wrong? They have had this view for as long as human beings have existed; it is inside them, it is them, it has been enrooted deep in their bones, they are born with this inner understanding.

CELL: But I reiterate that you have not a shred of proof to back up your case. You talk of inner feeling. Inner feeling, yes it is important in life, but it is no proof. Waking up one day and saying "I know something new" without being taught is utterly ridiculous.

SOUL: You have defied understanding. Are you to tell me that the human being is made of meat, that our consciousness is just a by-product of genetic mutation, that we are nothing but mimes?

CELL: And are you to tell me that the human was placed on Earth by an immortal flying thing that claims to be superior to all others by divine right? This "divine" creature must have had a foul fondness for cockroaches, a fondness that exceeds all limits of imagination.

SOUL: Your insolence has no bounds. You say that the human being is just an instruction manual and operating system of meat, just a meaningless bunch of meat. How can you think this?

CELL: Your stupidity is unmatched in the entire cosmos. You idiotic pig.

SOUL: I am not the idiotic pig; you are the idiotic pig. No you are worse than an idiotic pig; you are idiotic fly excrement.

CELL: How dare you, you piece of....

Our humanity gives us the gift of option. To respect your neighbors' opinions as if they were your own shows not only respect, but increases the chances of your opinions being accepted, for a person with a higher level of maturity is more likely to be correct. But to force your views on another is to show no respect, and thus your own views must be questioned, for they come from someone of less maturity.

YOU'RE TELLING MY KIDS THEY CAN'T READ THIS BOOK?

8-STUDENTS FIGHT: I WAS A BANNED JOURNALIST & BOARD MEMBER

MCPEARL is a Monroe County, New York, coalition working to keep public funds for public schools only. MCPEARL is dedicated to the protection of free public education, open to all children; and committed to the preservation of religious liberty as guaranteed by both the Federal and state constitutions.... Government support of private schools weakens the public schools. Private schools select their students. They choose the brighter and best-behaved and return children with learning and behavior problems to the public schools. The public schools then must deal with a disproportionate number of children who are difficult to teach and whose presence creates a poorer learning atmosphere for all children.

—United States Congress. Senate. "Statement of Monroe Citizens for Public Education and Religious Liberty, Martha Laties, Chairman," 1978

"Marty! Marty!" my father interrupts, urging my mother to lower her voice. We're eating dinner and my mother, having warmed to her favorite subject is talking louder and faster. I am nine years old, and I know all about her battle to keep taxpayer money from paying for private schools, as well as her efforts to keep prayer out of public schools.

My mom's opponents are well-known names in my house, chief among them, the columnist Father Andrew Greeley and the Congressman Barber Conable. The man she reveres, whose work I know up to the minute, is Leo Pfeffer, legal counsel for National PEARL.

My mother runs the local branch, MCPEARL, which stands for Monroe Citizens for Public Education and Religious Liberty. It has a few hundred members. When kids ask, I explain that she is a civic activist. What that means is, she organizes meetings, does research, writes letters to newspaper editors, publishes newsletters, travels to lobby legislators in Albany, and occasionally appears on TV.

The research: she gathers enrollment data from every school in the county and then, classroom by classroom, adds up—in pencil, on graph paper—the numbers of special education students at each school. Every year, this proves private schools have way fewer special ed kids than public schools. That is just one reason public taxes should not be paying for private schools: because private schools aren't accepting all the students who want to attend.

My mother specialized in ferreting out—election after election—what every school board candidate in the county truly believed. All these candidates, for decades, received detailed questionnaires from her. If they didn't respond, she'd telephone, and telephone again. Many candidates used evasive language; she worked hard to pin them down. Finally, she'd compile all candidates' responses to all questions and report these opinions in the MCPEARL newsletter.

Her letters to the editor were often published; sometimes the paper would add a paragraph warning readers she was the leader of an advocacy group.

After ten years specializing in battling to keep taxpayer money from private and religious schools, she broadened her scope and started fighting the teaching of Creationism in public schools.

Creationism had been pretty-well excluded from public school curricula decades before. As far back as the 1920's, the famous Scopes trial in Tennessee had marked a turning point. Creationism was understood in most of the nation to represent a backward way of thinking. But the rise of the Religious Right and a new wave of Evangelical Christianity in the mid-1970's was precursor to a revived effort to cast evolution as "just a theory" and Creationism as an equivalent theory that needed to be taught alongside.

If this had been a public discourse at the national level, there would have been no way for Creationists to overcome the scientific consensus in favor of evolution. But what my mother and her associates started noticing, in the mid-70's was the arrival of a new tactic, which was hyper-local.

People who want to run for school board must live in the district. We lived in western New York, outside of Rochester. Lots of school board candidates started popping up, whose families had recently moved to town. These transplants were coming from states some distance away, and they were right-wingers. When they received my mother's questionnaires, asking their views on taxpayer money going to private schools, or the teaching of Creationism, they were particularly vague. But when she got them on the phone or talked directly to them at candidates' forums—she organized lots of these, too—the truth was clear. This group of families had been prepped and assisted in relocating to our region, specifically to, first infiltrate, and then, take over school boards. It was a highly organized strategy to get Creationism into the curriculum and displace the teaching of evolution.

After a few years, it became evident that the strategy worked. Few people step forward to run for school board; few people turn out to vote in school board elections. These newcomers, who tactically moved into specific school districts, were able to win seats, and then become presidents of their boards.

Once they were lodged on their school boards, they'd begin to advance their pro-Creationist agenda, and, again, they seemed to have a carefully planned method of pushing for an approach to the teaching of evolution that emphasized it was just a theory.

In the 1970's, my mother's side had some big victories. The New York legislature, the US Congress, and the Supreme Court came down clearly against taxpayer money going to private and religious schools. But by the mid-1980's, it was clear that some of these gains were in danger of erosion, because of counterattacks from the religious right—known at that time as the Moral Majority.

I had grown up by then, and opened The Children's Bookstore, in Chicago. Of course I was on my mother's mailing list, and every few months her MCPEARL newsletter would arrive. When I visited my parents with my young family in tow, my mother would catch me up on her current battles.

Decades later, in 2020—just a few months before she died—I was visiting my mother at my sister's house in

Maryland. There was news coverage of a Supreme Court decision approving taxpayer-funded vouchers—a way for public taxes to fund private and religious schools. My mother cried out, "But we already won this fight!"

Apparently not: today's Supreme Court majority continues to boost the influence of religious belief on public schools, as shown most recently by their June 2025 *Mahmoud v. Taylor* ruling conferring on parents a religiously-based right to opt children out of story hours that include books with LGBTQ+ themes. Justice Sonia Sotomayor, in dissent, expressed concern that

> Many school districts...cannot afford to engage in costly litigation over opt-out rights.... Schools may instead censor their curricula, stripping material that risks generating religious objections. The Court's ruling, in effect, thus hands a subset of parents the right to veto curricular choices long left to locally elected school boards.

The fight to keep religion from shaping public school curricula must continue.

This current round of book-banning is part of the same long-term right-wing strategy first implemented to advance Creationism in the 1970's. A few people—a "subset of parents"—confidently take on a community that doesn't agree with them, and they succeed because they have the guidance of national organizations, and because not many people vote in school board elections:

> The majority of book censorship attempts are now originating from organized movements. Pressure groups

and government entities that include elected officials, board members, and administrators initiated 72% of demands to censor books in school and public libraries
—America Library Association, 2025

***

I became an outspoken kid at age nine—and lots of my classmates didn't like it. But as I grew up and had as my opponent the school principal—who they didn't like either—my classmates started to appreciate me, and I had lots of friends. That's when I became a banned teen journalist and got elected student representative to the school board. Here's how I tell the story in my self-published memoir, *The Music Thief:*

1968
Every night at dinner we watched the six o'clock news with Walter Cronkite. It was the Vietnam War, direct from the battlefield: helicopters, guns, explosions; villagers and soldiers wounded and killed.

Walter Cronkite started by saying how many: "One-thousand-four-hundred-and-twenty North Vietnamese dead. Eight-hundred-and-seventy-one Viet Cong dead. One-hundred-and-nineteen South Vietnamese dead. Forty-two Americans dead." The numbers were always in the same order, and they showed a lot more people on the North Vietnamese side were being killed than on the South Vietnamese, so our side was winning. I didn't know how so many Vietnamese could be killed but more could still be left.

There were interviews with American generals about how the US Army was keeping the North Vietnamese out of South Vietnam. The problem was the Viet Cong. These were

Communists who lived in South Vietnam. They fought by sneaking out of tunnels and killing Americans from behind.

One time, Walter Cronkite said the war wasn't going right. It was different, that night when he told what he really thought. My family agreed: Mommy wanted Gene McCarthy for president, so we'd get out of Vietnam.

As 1968 went on—with the assassinations of Martin Luther King and Robert Kennedy, who were on our side of civil rights, and then, with the anti-war protests at the Chicago Democratic Convention, where police beat up long-haired students—I developed strong opinions about who I was in the world.

That summer, I grew my hair long against the Vietnam War. By the time I started fourth grade this protest had made me look like a girl and earned me the insult, "Laties is a lady," and the names homo and faggot. Some kids did ask why my hair was long; when I said I was protesting the Vietnam War, they yelled I was a Commie hippie.

On the school bus, kids would call me out, saying I had to meet them in the woods. I'd refuse because I was in favor of peace. They'd call me a sissy.

At one point, I counted forty-eight nasty nicknames. When they'd start in, I'd rattle off all the names they'd invented back in their faces. I'd say I was reminding them, so they wouldn't skip any.

I also worked out a way of staring at them without blinking—like Max in *Where the Wild Things Are*. No matter what they said, I'd keep staring.

1975
The principal decided too many kids were in the hallways while classes were in session and announced a policy

requiring any student to have a signed pass permitting them to move between rooms. A bunch of my friends circulated a flyer titled *Screw the Pass,* featuring a picture of a screw (the kind you use with a screwdriver) going through a kid's head. There were two paragraphs of complaints about the policy.

Screw the Pass had been written and printed by members of the track team. The principal didn't know this. He suspended Brian Cooper, one of the school's few Black students, on the basis of having been caught passing out the flyer.

I wasn't involved. I was already the news editor of *Upper Story*—the regular school newspaper—and writing about the stupid rules. But the night of Brian Cooper's suspension, a bunch of us got t-shirts made that said, on the front: "Free Brian Cooper," and on the back "Screw the Pass." I wore mine all day. None of my teachers asked me to cover it up— which I took to be a sign of sympathy.

The vice principal pulled me out of chemistry class and when I refused to put on a sweater over the t-shirt, he brought me down to the principal's office.

The principal had concluded that I was the one behind the whole flyer thing. He accused me directly, and when I said I hadn't known it was going to happen, but I agreed with the flyer, he said I must know who had done it—and I said I did. He said this proved I was responsible.

I stated, "Just because I know an elephant has big ears, doesn't mean I put the big ears on the elephant."

The principal leapt to his feet, slammed his palm on his desk, and shouted, "Suspended! He's suspended! Call his mother!"

Mom drove me home, and said, "A man's reach should exceed his grasp, or what's a heaven for?" Her support was great.

The track-team journalists maintained secrecy, even as they enlisted more authors, and pumped out frequent underground newspapers. The administration was going nuts. Meanwhile, since I'd been suspended, I became a revolutionary celebrity. Even the kids who'd been harassing me since fourth grade about my long hair started encouraging me to keep fighting with the principal. A few months later, I ran for student representative to the school board and won.

The ringleaders graduated, so a bunch of us figured we'd better take up the slack. While the first year, the underground paper had been called *FightBack,* we decided to strike a more positive note. We called it *FightForward.*

I was also on the school board, and I sat on the dais with the adult board members. I was allowed to talk during the meetings. Some of the members clearly didn't like me, but some were sympathetic: two of my fellow jazz-band members' mothers were on the board. It was from one of them that I found out the superintendent was slandering me in executive session. My friend's mother called and asked, did I have a master key to the school, and was I going in at night? I certainly did not have a master key. I hung around whenever I wanted, though: several custodians were my friends. But I didn't want to be there except to play jazz, and go to student council meetings, and do theater, and play chess—well, yes, I was there a lot. More than the administration liked.

I seemed to be making those guys nervous. I'd developed a relationship with the Rochester branch of the American Civil Liberties Union. Also, Mom had taught me how to do research downtown, in a law library.

I'd used the ACLU once already. In eleventh grade I'd decided America was not the home of liberty and justice for all, so I'd started refusing to say the Pledge of Allegiance. My homeroom teacher had complained to the principal about my not standing up, and my silence. When the principal had threatened to discipline me, I'd spoken with the ACLU, and director Loren Warboys had sent a letter to the high school that laid out my right to remain silent during the Pledge.

I'd agreed with the vice principal on a compromise: I would wait outside the homeroom door each morning until the other students had said the Pledge, then I'd enter and take my seat for the attendance taking.

Especially after this experience, I was confident in exercising my constitutionally protected civil liberties in school.

FightForward had three themes: administration bullying, student apathy, and freedom of speech. Because the principal was trying to make us submit to his editing, before we distributed, and because I didn't conceal that this year, I was part of the project, it was a more straightforward fight for him than it had been the year before, when he hadn't known he was fighting the track team.

Our secret weapon was our parents' aid: especially our editor Mitch Ahern's access to his father's high-speed Ektaprint 225 copy machine—then in development at Kodak Corporation—which enabled us to produce two-thousand copies of the six-page paper, six times during the 76/77 school year, at no expense.

People would ask, "Are you really gonna sue the principal?" If he punished us severely, we were. The Supreme Court ruled against our side fifteen years later, but at the time, the law was with us. School administrators weren't allowed to enforce rules that said students had to submit newspapers for review before distribution. Also, the principal was allowed to punish us after we'd distributed only if what we'd said was libel, that is, actual lies. The ACLU was ready to sue, and our paper often focused on what the administration had done during the previous distribution. It made great copy.

Distributing was so much fun. The teachers had been told that if they saw any sign that one of our papers was being distributed, they should seize the copies and tell the main office, so additional teachers could be told to intervene. We'd have ten students enter the school by different entrances, each carrying two-hundred copies of *FightForward*. These ten had each lined up ten friends to whom they'd pass off twenty papers. These hundred would run around and give away twos and fives and tell people to pass them on. Naturally, when distribution was in progress, kids were grabbed by teachers, but it was usually with a small number of papers. The administration never succeeded in preventing a full-school distribution—it only took twenty minutes.

FightForward was read much more avidly than the official *Upper Story* paper.

The hubbub in Penfield caused the *Rochester Times-Union* to write an article about us, in which the vice principal was quoted referring to *FightForward's* editors as a group of "so-called pseudo-intellectuals." We loved that.

In May, our writer Matt Perry handed me a lengthy, inflammatory, and profound piece for the graduation issue of *FightForward*. We published "The Right to Your Rights" unedited.

It started off with a bang:

"Where are you going without a pass?"

"You can't go out there. Come in here. You're not supervised."

"Where were you yesterday? You weren't on the absentee bulletin."

"Where are your white socks?"

FUCK YOU.

Fuck you a hundred times and stick it up your ass sideways. That's what you would like to say to the people who ask you that type of question, especially if it is one of The Big Three Buffoons. But instead you say some bullshitty thing and walk away with your palms still sweating cause Christ almighty you almost got in trouble for doing something you weren't supposed to do....

Then, Matt transitioned to a psychology of ethics:

Being punished by your parents when you were young, and even now, is a method of imposing what they think is right or wrong on your mind. This is how you come to develop a moral code, what you think is right and what is wrong. When you punish someone for doing something wrong, you're attempting to take part of his mind and make it think the way you do....

What is right and what is wrong is relative. What I think is right might not be what you think is right....

Think about it. Is walking down the hall of a building so wrong? Is going outside of the building and sitting in the shade so bad? Is cutting class such a sin that the kid must be removed from school, abridging his right to learn? Is preventing a child from graduating high school because he did not complete a certain number of gym classes justified?...

Matt concluded with a rousing call for individual transformation:

Don't feel guilty about such silly things as leaving the school illegally, not using hall passes and wearing something other than those goddamn white socks. When you get rid of your guilt feelings about these and other trivial rules then you will have made the first step out of this wretched mess called Penfield High School.

For the year's final school board meeting, a vote was scheduled on whether to end the prior review rule for student publications. Most of the board members had told me they planned to vote yes, as a sort of present to me for having done a good job as student representative.

But Matt's article—in the issue of *FightForward* we'd distributed the day before the meeting—infuriated the board members. Several made speeches saying they now agreed with the principal that students couldn't be trusted to show good judgment in their publishing decisions. I answered that if the content of one offensive—but in no way libelous—article could interfere with the board's resolve to abide by the United States Constitution's First Amendment free speech guarantee, then a board vote to lift the prior review rule would have been meaningless in any case. They'd probably have reinstated the rule in the fall.

After the meeting, board member Clint Hutto cut loose at me, demanding how I could show such disrespect for the principal. I said, "I didn't write that article, but I support the author's right to express his opinion. Supreme Court Justice Oliver Wendell Holmes said, 'We should be eternally vigilant against attempts to check the expression of opinions that we loathe.'"

Hutto snorted and walked away.

A week later, the students elected Matt Perry to be their next student representative to the school board.

9-BOOKSELLERS FIGHT: CONVENING A COMMUNITY BOOK FESTIVAL

Easton Book Festival's mission is to inform, educate, enrich and inspire people of all backgrounds in our community through cultural and literary programs and to otherwise foster intellectual discourse and civic engagement.
—Mission Statement of Easton Book Festival

Nothing fights book banning as effectively as "more speech." This means book festivals, because even though many people never enter a bookstore or library, they all can be reached with a book festival.

***

"Doesn't it seem with all these local festivals every year— Garlicfest, Baconfest, Heritage Day—Easton could have one around books? I want to launch Easton Literature Festival."

I'm chatting with State Representative Robert Freeman during the grand opening party for Book and Puppet Company, in September 2017. "I've been saying that for thirty years," Bob responds. "But it should be called Easton Book Festival."

It took time to get the bookstore running, but a year later I put out a call for festival volunteers; thirty regular customers showed up for a vigorous planning session. We ran the first Easton Book Festival in October 2019. Now, in Spring 2025, we're working on our seventh.

Here are some strategies we've developed to match the opportunity we have in this community:

1) **Convene a team of motivated leaders for your board.**

   We've never had more than five board members and they work a lot in the months before the festival. Most important is that they're available for all-hands-on-deck action during the festival itself. Also, three committee chairs pull a lot of weight, and thirty committee members help them.

2) **Invite program proposals from the public, using an online submission form.**

   We post a request-for-proposal button on our website several months before the festival. Here's the text (written by current board chair, Darrell Parry, of Lafayette College Bookstore):

   > *Description of Proposed Event*—We recommend multi-author curated readings, panel discussions, presentations or writing workshops. Single author readers can sign up for one of our open mic slots and bring books to sell. (see event listing for dates and times closer to October):
   > *Title of Proposed Event:*
   > *Titles of Featured Books:*

Names of Proposed Presenters and Authors—
Three or more readers or presenters preferred for
non-workshop events:
*Biographies of Proposed Presenters and
Authors:*
Anything Else We Should Know?:

3) Feature local writers, including self-published and unpublished authors.

We are not a festival that showcases well-known
authors touring to support their new books, released
by big publishers. Instead, we are a radically
inclusive community celebration of writing.

So many people write!

During a three-day festival, we run five open mic
events. Our most successful is "Wicked Brew," when
any writer can share Halloween-themed work.
Another open mic is for local college students, two
more open mics showcase established local poetry
collectives, another open mic is completely free form.

Our genre panel discussions featuring local
authors are popular. Mystery, historical-fiction, and
romance are fiction topics that interest attendees.
Non-fiction author panels focus on local history,
memoir, and hot-button controversies.

4) Run a Small Press Expo.

We rent a downtown museum's conference room to
host forty local small presses and self-published
authors, who display their books on 6-foot tables
during a half-day vendor fair. Hundreds of people
come to chat with authors and buy their books.

5) Send authors into schools.
The way to reach every family in town is to bring authors into all schools. This is our big expense: we must hire authors who are good at presenting to two-hundred-fifty kids, a skill many authors haven't mastered. Schools won't work with us again if we send authors who can't handle the kids!

Ask around for recommendations for who to hire: all over the country there are children's authors skilled at working in the schools.

Sometimes you can pay a reduced fee if you guarantee some book sales.

6) Run children's programs at the library, on the Monday of a three-day weekend.
This is a great location and day for a public series of children's-author programs. Also, we have a volunteer wear a children's-book character costume like Clifford, which we rent from Costume Specialists, in Columbus, Ohio.

7) Publish a color newsprint booklet listing programs, and featuring sponsor ads.
We post the program schedule on our website, and we hire an agency to help us successfully advertise on social media—but also we print three-thousand copies of a thirty-two page "penny-saver"-style booklet. The booklet gives us a way to publish ads from local businesses whose contributions help pay our expenses. We leave stacks of these program booklets at a hundred local coffee shops, libraries,

hardware stores, museums and community centers—
and we give out program booklets during the festival.

***

Facebook comment from a festival volunteer:
Who would believe that last night, outside of Pearly
Bakers, was a group of guys clutching their pearls about
the Easton Book Festival brochure that I had left there?
What had caught their attention was the Drag Queen
Story Hour.

One guy in particular—in a group of six—was upset
about the sexualizing of children, via the Drag Queen
Story Hour. As I arrived, he was appealing to his friends
to call out this depravity.

It was mentioned, by a staff member, that it was me
that had put the offending brochure there.

All eyes turned to me.

Seriously, I said, you want to talk about Drag Queen
Story Hour, instead of Ben Franklin giving The Rights of
Man Speech made so famous by Thomas Paine thirty
years later? Yes, Thomas Paine.

Thomas Paine was a name that was vaguely familiar
but none of them could actually place him. I suggested
there were many things about the Easton Book Festival
to marvel at, and it seemed to me that fixating on the
Drag Queen Story Hour was an odd choice.

"And by the way guys, there is zero sexual content or
sexual innuendo in the Drag Queen Story Hour."

What, they demanded!

I repeated it adamantly several times.

It's simply about letting kids know that they can be who they want to be.

I used the examples of men not being allowed to grow long hair, when I was a young man, or women being allowed to wear pants, not too many decades ago. They agreed that they like their long hair etc.

The moment passed! They went on their way very much calmed down.

—M.J. King

***

Email exchange with author:
Hey Artie—I have bad news.

Monday our committee met with the school district people who are booking the classroom programming, and yesterday I learned that they didn't want you.

They said that the children would go home and tell their parents that they'd been learning about poop in school.

This is a pretty good reminder that we are in Trump country, as of 2016. I was pretty shocked.

Anyway, this did happen.

I guess—does this happen to you very much? We are having a children's book censorship panel discussion at 4:30pm on Sat Oct 26 and I wonder if you would come onto that panel.

I'm sorry this has happened.

Best, Andy

Hi, Andy. Oh my, that's mighty disappointing. No, it's actually never happened before. The books are packed

with fun science, wordplay, gentle humor, multiculturalism. They're not at all gross or offensive....
—Artie Bennett, author, *Poopendous,* (and lots of other great books)

***

In celebration of the breakthrough collective biography, *The Trials of Mumia Abu-Jamal: A Biography in 25 Voices,* the book's editor Todd Steven Burroughs talked with moderator Melba Tolliver—our book festival's former board chair—along with Mumia Abu-Jamal's spiritual advisor Mark Taylor, Baruch College Professor of History Johanna Fernandez, and the publisher of Mumia's comix, Seth Tobocman of *World War 3 Illustrated.*
—*Youtube* video description

Mumia Abu-Jamal, Philadelphia's acclaimed public-radio broadcaster, joined our 2022 panel discussion from prison. Known worldwide as a political prisoner—there's a street named Rue Mumia Abu-Jamal in the Paris suburb of Saint-Denis—Abu-Jamal was transferred off death row in response to an international human rights campaign. Now, he is serving a life sentence.

At the time of his 1982 conviction for killing a police officer—an accusation Abu-Jamal denies—he'd been an award-winning investigative journalist. In prison, Mumia has written eleven books, including *Live from Death Row.* So, in Easton, Pennsylvania, he's a regional author.

For our session, Johanna Fernandez—earlier that day—had recorded Mumia's comments, via telephone. She played aloud the audio of his relaxed baritone voice:

When Professor Fernandez—Johanna—first told me about Easton, Pennsylvania, a light went on in my head. It's a distant memory. Unless I'm just going crazy, I believe that Easton was the home of the heavyweight champion of the United States, a guy named Larry Holmes. He fought some pretty spectacular fights back in the old days.

In the old days, you remember when someone got into the ring, what's the first thing they said? The announcer would always say, "And coming from the great city of..." He would say the city, and then he would name the fight, "Easton, P.A., Larry Holmes in this corner."

That's where it rings in my head. This great fighter, and me watching as a boxing fan. That's probably the extent [laughs] of anything I can recall about Easton, but it's pretty remarkable.

Larry Holmes put Easton on the map, at least the recent mental map of what Pennsylvania looks like outside of the big city of Philadelphia, and Pittsburgh. There you have it. That's what Easton means to me.

Hopefully, I think after today, it'll mean something else. I certainly hope so.

So, in this corner is Easton, Pennsylvania. Who knew that in Easton, there would be a book fair?

It appears to me that in places like Easton, in places that most people really haven't heard about or really haven't visited, are people, just like us, around a table, gathering together in a small community center, reading.

I think this is a time to read, to think, to imagine a new world, a new America, and a new lease on life in a country that is, I think, going in the wrong direction and traveling down the road of fascism.

When people think together, when they work together, when they even breathe together, change is possible. Because it takes ideas to move the world.

So, I'm glad to hear about this book festival. As a writer, [laughs] I love book festivals.

Keep on keeping on, keep on reading, keep on transforming the world.

With love, not fear, this is Mumia Abu-Jamal.

YOU'RE TELLING MY KIDS THEY CAN'T READ THIS BOOK?

10-CONCLUSION: WHY WE MUST WIN THE FIGHT FOR FREEDOM TO READ

Published simultaneously in Paris, Geneva, Amsterdam, London and Brussels on 22 February 1759, [*Candide*] soon became *the* bestseller of the European book trade in the eighteenth century. Cramer, its Genevan publisher, printed an initial run of 2,000 copies, the norm for a book that was expected to sell well: within a month, after further printings and many pirated editions, at least 20,000 copies had been sold. After a similar period even Swift's *Gulliver's Travels* (published 28 October 1726) had sold only half that number...

The original publication of *Candide* was a carefully calculated coup. Unbound copies of the work (in pocketbook duodecimo format) were discreetly dispatched from Geneva on 15 and 16 January 1759; 1,000 to Paris, 200 to Amsterdam, and the others to London and Brussels. They were then bound at their respective destinations and published on a previously agreed date, the idea being to circulate as many copies of the original edition as possible throughout Europe before pirated editions usurped and corrupted it (and, in those days before the laws of international copyright, siphoned off Voltaire's potential profits). The aim, too, was to create the maximum stir in as many countries as possible before the authorities could suppress this subversive tale. In the event, although the police were quick to seize all the copies they could and to smash any press on which a new edition was being printed, the flood was too great for them to stem. The damage was done—before the Vatican got round to placing *Candide* on its Index of forbidden books on 24 May 1762.

—Roger Pearson, "Introduction," in Voltaire, *Candide and Other Stories*

History teaches that today's American efforts to keep readers from books are nonsensical: because of the Internet, more books are more accessible to more people than ever before. Yet, still, as Robie Harris explains,

> Not every challenge means the book is taken out of that library. But it may be. And then who really suffers from that? Those children who may come to the library...who are either looking for something specific that they need to read about, to help them go through their lives— normal healthy lives—or sometimes when there are very disturbing things....
>
> Or they come across a book by happenstance. And they read it, and they say, "Oh, that's me."

Children who don't discover the books they need, in their school libraries, must find them later, elsewhere. Our job—as parents and neighbors—is to ensure this happens. My colleagues and I have devoted our lives to this effort.

This decade's dramatic confrontations among community members—confrontations engineered by national right-wing organizations—serve to divert citizens' attention from those groups' much larger efforts to dismantle American democracy.

We must prevent them from succeeding, by sharing our voices.

Writing and publishing are how we can learn from one another, to collaboratively build our nation's next era.

When we read each other's books, we suspend disbelief and agree to disagree.

The joy of reading is this personal transformation.

YOU'RE TELLING MY KIDS THEY CAN'T READ THIS BOOK?

ACKNOWLEDGMENTS

For inspiration and encouragement, I thank Eric and Bobbie Carle, Nick and Trinkett Clark, Robie Harris, Carl Lennertz, Tiffany Yates Martin, Gloria Jean and Jerry Pinkney, Zena Sutherland, Melba Tolliver, and Jack Zipes.

I thank friends and colleagues about whom I tell stories here: Mumia Abu-Jamal, Mitch Ahern, Mira Bartok, Artie Bennett, Joan Bertin, Christine Bluhm, Aron Boks and Marie, John Borden, Allie Jane Bruce, Todd Steven Burroughs, Brian Cooper, Stacy Creamer, Emily Danforth, Elizabeth Dickey, Michael Emberley, Johanna Fernandez, Robert Freeman, David Gale, Paul Gulino, Carla Hayden, Kirsten Yauch Hess, Sander Hicks, Larry Holmes, Cheryl Willis Hudson, Wade Hudson, Clint Hutto, M.J. King, Ginny Moore Kruse, Valerie Lewis, Leonard Marcus, NAIBA colleagues, George Nicholson, Darrell Parry, Matt Perry, Connie Porter, Beth Puffer, David Reuther, B.J. Richards, Justin Richardson, Karen Rizzo, Dan Simon, John Steptoe, Roger Sutton, Seth Tobocman, Valerie Tripp, Tomi Ungerer, Loren Warboys, Cynthia Weill, Ama Karikari Yawson, and Phoebe Yeh. I hope I represented events accurately.

For love throughout my life, I thank Sarah and Sam Laties, Martha and Victor Laties, Nancy Laties Feresten and Tim Feresten, Claire Laties Davis and Ty Davis, David Laties, Sylvan Migdal and Jessica Spears, and Curtis and Otis Whitear.

For support, forbearance and love, I thank my soulmate, Gaia Abraxas.

Further information and advice about today's censorship crisis can be found in American Booksellers Association's outstanding 2024 publication, *The ABA Right to Read Handbook: Fighting Book Bans and Why It Matters.*

YOU'RE TELLING MY KIDS THEY CAN'T READ THIS BOOK?

NOTES

PRELUDE—ASSIGNMENT FROM MELBA

Page 1. Melba Tolliver. *Accidental Anchorwoman*. Easton, PA: Rebel Bookseller, 2024.

Page 1. Elizabeth DeOrnellas, "Supporters, opponents mark day," *Morning Call*, January 21, 2025.

Page 1. George Lakoff. *Don't Think of an Elephant! Know Your Values and Frame the Debate*. White River Junction, VT: Chelsea Green Publishing, 2004.

Page 2. "AR-15 rifles"
I later learned the second-day bookseller hadn't known the exact story. Here is how the original bookseller explained the presence of rifles to me, in an email, "A number of men showed up carrying AR-15 rifles in front of the store to counter-protest a Black Lives Matter event. This...really raised the level of concern for bookseller safety, since the groups backing the gun-toting individuals also openly attacked the store...on social media."

Page 3. Justin Richardson and Peter Parnell. *And Tango Makes Three*. Illustrated Henry Cole. New York: Simon & Schuster, 2005.

1—BABA GOES TO THE LIBRARY

Page 6. Bill Martin, Jr. *Brown Bear, Brown Bear, What Do You See?* Illustrated by Eric Carle. New York: Doubleday & Co., 1967.

Page 7. Andrew Laties. *Rebel Bookseller: How to Improvise Your Own Indie Store and Beat Back the Chains*. New York: Vox Pop, 2005. Andrew Laties. *Rebel Bookseller: Why Indie Businesses Represent Everything You Want to Fight For—From Free Speech, to Buying Local, to Building Communities*. Second Edition. New York: Seven Stories Press, 2011. I tell the tale of how Vox Pop came to publish *Rebel Bookseller* in my 2009 unpublished memoir, *Vox Pop, Sander, and Me:* "Vox Pop's founder Sander Hicks had published the biography of George W. Bush that told of a 1972 arrest for cocaine use while driving—an arrest all record of which was quashed and expunged by father George H.W. Bush. The book, *Fortunate Son,* written by James Hatfield, was first printed in a seventy-five thousand copy print-run, then—after intimidation from the George W. Bush presidential campaign—recalled and incinerated by its publisher St.

Martin's Press. Sander Hicks's company Soft Skull Press had obtained the rights after this recall, and republished the book, surviving lawsuits and publicity debacles to see the information distributed. (The key anecdote's source turned out to be close George W. Bush friend Karl Rove, who'd told Hatfield the story personally, and never denied having done so. However, Hatfield ended up a suicide.) If anyone was qualified to handle my book, it was surely this man who'd seen an unpublishable book into print, even though he'd lost control of his company while doing so." The tale of Sander Hicks publishing *Fortunate Son* was made into the 2002 documentary *Horn & Halos,* by filmmakers Suki Hawley and Michael Galinsky.

Page 9. Ezra Jack Keats. *The Snowy Day*. New York: The Viking Press, 1962.

Page 9. John Steptoe. *Stevie*. New York: Harper and Row, 1969.

Page 9. John Steptoe. *Mufaro's Beautiful Daughters*. New York: Scholastic, 1987.

Page 10. Merri V. Lindgren, Megan Schliesman, Tessa Michaelson Schmidt, and Madeline Tyner, "CCBC and Diverse Books: Numbers Are Just Part of the Story," *The Horn Book Magazine,* May 08, 2023. https://www.hbook.com/story/ccbc-and-diverse-books-numbers-are-just-part-of-the-story

Page 12. Leonard S. Marcus. "Eric Carle: Born June 25, 1929, Syracuse, New York," *Ways of Telling: Conversations on the Art of the Picture Book*. New York: Penguin, 2002. 40-41.

Page 13. Eric Carle. *The Artist Who Painted a Blue Horse*. New York: Penguin, 2011.

2—PUBLISHERS FIGHT

Page 17. Connie Porter. *Meet Addy*. Middleton, WI: Pleasant Company, 1993.

Page 17. Blogpost: "American Girl Historical Books Banned in Florida Schools," February 3, 2023. https://www.americangirldollnews.com/post/american-girl-historical-books-banned-in-florida-schools

Page 18. Wade Hudson and Cheryl Willis Hudson, Editors. *We Rise, We Resist, We Raise Our Voices*. New York: Crown Books for Young Readers, 2018.

Page 19. Cheryl Willis Hudson. *Afro-Bets ABC Book*. West Orange, NJ: Just Us Books, 1987.

3—EDUCATORS FIGHT

Page 23: The Bank Street Center for Children's Literature, which is led by Cynthia Weill, created this day of discussion. All four sessions can be viewed on Bank Street Library's Youtube channel: https://www.youtube.com/@bankstreetlibrary

The session titles are:

"Who Are You to Say? Panel 1: Children's Literature and the Censorship Conversation, April 16, 2016,"

"Who Are You to Say? Panel 2: Children's Literature and the Censorship Conversation, April 16, 2016,"

"Who Are You to Say? Panel 3: Children's Literature and the Censorship Conversation, April 16, 2016,"

"Who Are You to Say? Keynote: Children's Literature and the Censorship Conversation, April 16, 2016."

Page 24. "We must remain eternally vigilant not to suppress the expression of opinions that we loathe."—Justice Holmes dissenting in *Abrams v. United States,* 1919.

Page 26. Robie Harris. *It's Perfectly Normal*. Illustrated by Michael Emberley. Somerville, MA: Candlewick Press, 1994.

Page 26. Emily Danforth. *The Miseducation of Cameron Post*. New York: Balzer + Bray, 2012.

Page 27. Andrew Laties, "At the Bookstore, An Exciting Path Ahead," Bank Street College website, June 8, 2012. www.bankstreet.edu.

Page 30. *"Bank Street Readers"*

"1965: The first multiethnic urban basal readers, the *Bank Street Reader*s revolutionize early childhood literacy. They are conceived by President John Niemeyer, written by Publications Division staff, and led by director Irma Simonton Black."—https://www.bankstreet.edu/about-bank-street/history/

Page 31. Lucy Sprague Mitchell. *Here and Now Storybook*. New York: E.P. Dutton, 1921.

Page 31. "Bank Street Writers Lab"

Margaret Wise Brown. *The Runaway Bunny*. Illustrated by Clement Hurd. New York: Harper and Row, 1942. Margaret Wise Brown. *Goodnight Moon*. Illustrated by Clement Hurd. New York: Harper and Row, 1947. Crockett Johnson. *Harold and the Purple Crayon.* New York: Harper and Row, 1955. Ruth Krauss. *The Carrot Seed.* Illustrated by Crockett Johnson. New York: Harper and Row, 1945. Leonard Marcus. *Golden Legacy: The Story of Golden Books.* New York: Golden Books, 2017. Maurice Sendak. *Where the Wild Things Are.* New York: Harper and Row, 1963.

4—AUTHORS FIGHT

Page 33. Helen Bannerman. *The Story of Little Black Sambo.* London, 1899.

Page 33. May Hill Arbuthnot. *Children's Books Too Good to Miss.* Cleveland, OH: Press of Western Reserve University, 1948.

Page 34. Phyllis J. Yuill. *Little Black Sambo: A Closer Look. A History of Helen Bannerman's* The Story of Little Black Sambo *and its Popularity/Controversy in the United States.* New York: Racism and Sexism Resource Center for Educators, 1976.

Page 35. Shirley Anne Tate. *Decolonising Sambo: Transculturation, Fungibility and Black and People of Colour Futurity, Second Edition.* Leeds, UK: Emerald Publishing, 2025. 61.

Page 35. Joseph Boskin. *Sambo: The Rise and Demise of an American Jester.* New York: Oxford University Press, 1986. 5-7.

Page 39. "If there be time to expose"
Justice Brandeis in *Whitney v. California, 1927.*

Page 39. Eric Rohmann. *My Friend Rabbit.* New York: Roaring Brook Press, 2002.

Page 43. "David Reuther didn't take that book"
David Reuther did publish other books of Jerry's, including *Noah's Ark* in 2002. Also.: Jerry Pinkney. *Aesop's Fables.* San Francisco, CA: SeaStar Books, 2000.

Page 44. "sympathetic, positive *Sambo*"
I have reworked my explanatory "quote" from Jerry Pinkney after discussing the book's origins with Gloria Jean Pinkney. Julius Lester. *Sam and the Tigers.* Ill. Jerry Pinkney. New York: Dial Press, 1996.

Page 44. Julius Lester. *The Tales of Uncle Remus: The Adventures of Br'er Rabbit.* Ill. Jerry Pinkney. New York: Dial Press, 1987.

Page 44. Jerry Pinkney. *The Lion & the Mouse.* New York: Little Brown and Co., 2009.

5—LIBRARIANS FIGHT

Page 47. Robert Sullivan, "Tomi Ungerer's Triumphant Return," *The New Yorker,* February 4, 2015.

Page 49. William Steig. *Sylvester and the Magic Pebble.* New York: Simon & Schuster, 1969.

Page 49. Judy Blume. *Are You There God? It's Me Margaret.* New York: Bradbury Press, 1970.

Page 49. Maurice Sendak. *In the Night Kitchen.* New York: Harper and Row, 1970.

Page 50. "ALA sponsored a petition"
Robert Sullivan, "Tomi Ungerer's Triumphant Return," *The New Yorker,* February 4, 2015.

Page 52. Zena Sutherland. *Children and Books, 6th Edition.* Northbrook, IL: Scott, Foresman and Company, 1981.

Page 54. "Position Statement includes providing"
American Association of School Librarians (AASL), "National School Library Standards for Learners, School Librarians, and School Libraries," Chicago: ALA, 2018. 54.

Page 54. Karoline Leavitt, "LIVE: White House Press Briefing," *ABC News,* May 9, 2025.

Page 54. Roger Sutton, "Making a Difference in Our Nation's Library: An Interview with Dr. Carla Hayden," *The Horn Book Magazine, May*/June 2018.

6—PARENTS FIGHT

Page 57. Ama Karikari Yawson. *Sunne's Gift.* New York: Milestales, 2014.

Page 59. "thirteen million books"
https://www.ingramcontent.com/retailers/products

Page 61. Dan Simon, email to Andrew Laties. April 5, 2018.

Page 62. Anonymous [Joe Klein]. *Primary Colors.* New York: Random House, 1996.

Page 63. Mira Bartok. *The Memory Palace.* New York: Free Press, 2011.

7—INTERLUDE

Page 65. Andrew Laties and Samuel Laties. *Son of Rebel Bookseller.* Easton, PA: Mythoprint, 2020.

8—STUDENTS FIGHT

Page 69. United States Congress. Senate. "Statement of Monroe Citizens for Public Education and Religious Liberty, Martha Laties, Chairman," 1978.

Page 73. "taxpayer-funded vouchers"
Espinoza v. Montana Department of Revenue, 2020

Page 73. Justice Sotomayor in *Mahmoud v. Taylor,* 2025

Page 73. "The majority of book censorship attempts"
"2024 Book Ban Data," American Library Association, 2025.
https://www.ala.org/bbooks/book-ban-data

Page 74. Andrew Laties. *The Music Thief.* Easton, PA: Mythoprint, 2020.

9—BOOKSELLERS FIGHT

Page 83. "Mission statement"
https://eastonbookfestival.com/about-us/

Page 87. "Facebook comment from a festival volunteer"
Facebook-post comment from Michael John King, October 22, 2022.

Page 89. Artie Bennett. *Poopendous.* Illustrated by Mike Moran. New York: Blue Apple Books, 2012.

Page 89. Todd Steven Burroughs. *The Trials of Mumia Abu-Jamal: A Biography in 25 Voices.* New York: Diasporic Africa Press, 2022.

Page 89. Easton Book Festival. *The Trials of Mumia Abu-Jamal"* *Panel Discussion.* Easton Book Festival Youtube channel, 2022.
https://www.youtube.com/@eastonbookfestival4827

Page 89. Mumia Abu-Jamal. *Live from Death Row.* New York: Harpercollins, 1996.

10—CONCLUSION

Page 93. Roger Pearson, "Introduction," in Voltaire, *Candide and Other Stories.* New York: Everyman's Library, 1992.

Page 94. "Who Are You to Say? Panel 1: Children's Literature and the Censorship Conversation, April 16, 2016," Bank Street Library.
https://www.youtube.com/@bankstreetlibrary

ACKNOWLEDGEMENTS

Page 97. American Booksellers Association and Philomena Polefrone. *The ABA Right to Read Handbook: Fighting Book Bans and Why It Matters,* 2024.

ANDREW LATIES co-founded Easton Book Festival, Book & Puppet Company, Vox Pop, The Children's Bookstore, Chicago Children's Museum Store, and The Eric Carle Museum Bookstore. He shared the 1987 Women's National Book Association's Pannell Award for bringing children and books together. His *Rebel Bookseller: Why Indie Businesses Represent Everything You Want to Fight For—From Free Speech to Buying Local to Building Communities* won the 2006 Independent Publisher Award and is available in a second edition from Seven Stories Press.

ALSO BY ANDREW LATIES

NONFICTION

Living Ur Sonata: Conjuring Kurt Schwitters to Transcend Authority and Seize the Hour

The Music Thief

Rebel Bookseller: Why Indie Businesses Represent Everything You Want to Fight For—From Free Speech to Buying Local to Building Communities

Son of Rebel Bookseller: A Very Large Homework Assignment

Which Way Up Is This? A Bookseller's Dream Journal

MUSIC

Three Fates Sing Ur Sonata
    —with Karl Berger, Ingrid Sertso, and Urchestra

Thou Art Continuous
    —with Eric Blitz

ALSO PUBLISHED BY REBEL BOOKSELLER

Accidental Anchorwoman: A Memoir of Chance, Choice, Change, and *Connection*
    —by Melba Tolliver